USTINOV STILL AT LARGE

Peter Ustinov

USTINOV
STILL AT
LARGE

Michael O'Mara Books Limited

First published in Great Britain in 1993 by
Michael O'Mara Books Limited
9 Lion Yard
Tremadoc Road
London SW4 7NQ

A CIP catalogue record for this book is available
from the British Library

ISBN 1-85479-134-6
Typeset by Florencetype Ltd,
Kewstoke, Avon
Printed in England by
Clays Ltd, St Ives plc

Sun Strokes High Anxieties

At last the sun has deigned to shine in summer, where it belongs. We are becoming used to all the weird quirks of the climate, which has us searching for symptoms like nervous peasants of the Middle Ages. Sudden heat-waves in midwinter, rain and even snow on relatively low peaks in August, what next? And we listen to the witchdoctors on television pontificating about the ozone layer, acid rain, and the hothouse effect, and we nod sagely, not really understanding all the implications, but seizing enough of the general drift to become anxious, to say the least.

In this atmosphere, the sunshine in summer is reassuring. And this, despite the fact that it is traditionally the time in which the great spoilsports of the recent past, the General Staffs of the Powers that were, chose to make war. The longer days meant that fighting could last almost twice as long as during winter, and with the added advantage of agreeable climatic conditions. The great virtue of the vernal season was that you could see your enemy practically round the clock, although there was an inherent risk in that, if things turned out badly, he could see you for the same length of time.

There was another consideration in these diabolical calculations, and that was the morale factor, especially important in fighting the French. There is no people which so clearly divides the working year from '*les vacances*', the vacations. It seems as though everyone lays down their tools virtually on the same day, in order to transfer the overcrowding of the cities on to the coastline. Then, on another prescribed day, they all evacuate

1

the coastline and reoccupy the cities, travelling like plagues of locusts; very slow locusts with generally bad tempers. There have been many official attempts to break up the regularity of this habit, but with only moderate success.

Anyone invading France in the past sought to deprive the population of these joys by attacking at the very moment of the exodus, and thus robbing it of hours of driving pleasure in traffic jams with children screaming and dogs barking, or similar infernos in trains. If the French resisted heroically, it was perhaps because the fathers of the households had been able to substitute the relative peace of the trenches for the horror of holidays.

Be that as it may, there is relatively little fighting going on in the world today, even if peace is, as ever, uneasy. A high summer without tourists has cast a gloomy shadow over Yugoslavia, and there are signs that the wastefulness and dimwittedness of civil war is being understood even among the most obtuse members of the governments and military. Of course, buildings destroyed by the impetuous and the trigger happy can be replaced, but it takes time, and, even more important in these days of economic uncertainty, money. There has to be at least a hesitation these days before destruction is indulged in as an instrument of policy.

What about the Gulf? Well even in that curious operation, while the intelligent bombs were wreaking their intelligent havoc, the industrial powers were jockeying for position in the reconstruction derby; first of all in Kuwait, later, if all goes badly, in Iraq. For some this was a Holy War. A minority, one would guess, who wished to recover their vandalized palaces. For others, it was a clean-cut war of good versus evil, as suggested by none other than President Bush. Yet others had reason to think of it as a huge public relations campaign in which the ailing motor of the United Nations was refuelled with high octane moral purpose, and given the romantic name of 'Desert Storm', worthy of Rudolf Valentino, but without his virtue of silence.

Until recently, nobody from the ranks of the sceptical had ever thought of it as an air-display. Now, the Swiss Government, of all hard-headed organizations, has ordered about forty American combat aircraft, preferring them to their French competitors, giving as a reason for their choice their brilliant performance in the Gulf War. Not only did the war have a commercial aspect — did it not start with a search for sponsors, like any other commercial enterprise? — but it will obviously stir a commercial interest in some of the hardware when this becomes available to all. It takes an expert to understand why Switzerland needs forty aircraft at this moment. To a rank layman like myself, forty seems either too many or too few. Obsolescence will rear its head before a decade is over, and then twenty aircraft will have to be invested in. Twenty because then they will cost slightly more than the forty do today. And they won't even be used except in fly-pasts on national holidays.

Meanwhile the sun is hot, the skies are blue. It is possible to dispense with the adornments of cities, such as ties and socks. Even shoes and shirts. All around, heavy industry on a scale of intimacy, wasps and bees behaving like giants in their own world, insects of many and obscure varieties struggling on their backs as they lie on the unperforated skin of the water in the pool, then panicking and threatening to sink. Oh, the feelings of piety as one rescues one drowning speck of life after another with the help of a leaf, or by using a finger as a landing pad. Perhaps it is here, in a pool, in close proximity to some of the smallest visible inhabitants of our planet, that one may reflect with profit on the value of life in general. And to think that somewhere there are those who say that any loss of life is tragic, while laying plans for hypothetical scenarios in terms of divisions and army corps, and permissible numbers of casualties! And what is the pretext for these contradictory, and in fact, incompatible thoughts? Summer.

3 August, 1991

Rich Cashing in on the Poor

Sociologists frequently point to the imbalances evident in the distribution of the world's wealth as the reasons for a potential explosion of the Third World's anger aimed at the greedy, arrogant First World and its undying pretensions. It is an often quoted fact that 20 per cent of the earth's population enjoys 80 per cent of its resources. It stands to reason that 80 per cent of the population has to be satisfied with 20 per cent of these resources. The imbalance is such that it can hardly fail to rankle. And it is underscored by the spread of a certain kind of corruption from the developed world, an import the developing world can scarcely relish.

Look at the broad face of Africa, if you will. The landscape has not changed much with the passage of the years, nor have the handmaidens of poverty—epidemic and famine. And yet the cities are different from what they were, boasting skyscrapers and status symbols: all the positive signs of concentrations of wealth in privileged places, and the sudden existence of big money and a social elite against the same old background of human misery. That constitutes the spread of free societies in our image. And in our eyes the creation of small versions of the large internal imbalances existing in our society will somehow lessen the gap between the haves and the have-nots. At worst, it will create a privileged caste with which the privileged in the West will be able to share a language. In fact, this erosion of traditional African and Asian values will not militate in our favour in the long run. It is certain that there exists a privileged minority of those able to govern in a more mature fashion than the sinister vaudeville figure of Idi

Amin and the equally atrocious Emperor Bokassa of the Central African Republic, the one a distortion of the British Imperial tradition, the other a caricature of Napoleon Bonaparte, with the emphasis on Waterloo. That Africa has already produced leaders of great vision and balanced judgment is undeniable. But the fact is that the nations outside the circle of the favoured few are gradually opting for the deployment of latter-day Robin Hoods to make their points for them, and to oppose the haughtiness of their old masters with weapons within their means. To us, in the developed world, Saddam Hussein is a figure no more endearing than Amin or Bokassa, and yet his ability to survive, to bluff, to strut and swagger in the most blatant of adversities, gives him the aura of an inspired bandit, a tweaker of noses. Unlike the real Robin Hood (if he ever really existed outside the realm of English legend and wishful thinking) Saddam may well rob the rich to make himself richer, but the end results are hardly in question here, merely the motives. Anyone who rises, or seems to rise, against the status quo achieved during a colonial past as the fruits of long forgotten victory is almost bound to have the support of those who do not have the riches of their soil to contribute, but merely the sweat of their brow. The wealth of the comparatively recent state of Kuwait is literally like inherited wealth in a family. The survival of countries like Jordan and Yemen have to be fought for by the ingenuity and industry of their citizens over-seas, who send at least part of their earnings home. It is natural that Kuwait possesses much more to interest the overdeveloped West than do the other two, or indeed Kurdistan, which has never been able to create a nation of its own accord. It is stretched like a worn blanket over five existing nations, and attracts attention only by affronts to our sense of humanity, a recent and most wel-come ingredient in an assessment of our own responsibilities.

Now, on quite a different level, but with the same principal players, comes the scandal of the Bank of Credit and Commerce International, described by the American prosecutor as the greatest fraud in the history of banking. Britain, true to itself, still seems to be dragging its feet while attempting to be scrupulous. The Secret Service and the Bank of England appear to have known for some time that Abu Nidal used the bank as a conduit for financing terrorist activities on a world scale. But, for fear of being precipitate, no one made a move until now. The Americans have fewer hang-ups. Where the security of a nation is concerned, or the integrity of banking, it is always safer to shoot first and apologize later, even to the next of kin, than to be left with egg on your face and a hole in your foot. The United States went as far as demanding the extradition of Mr Abedi, the founder of the bank, believed to have filled his pockets with billions of dollars. For the record, Mr Abedi is a Pakistani, living, not unnaturally, in Pakistan. If the allegations are true, he is another of the new generation of Robin Hoods. In this case he would have robbed the poor to make himself rich, but that matters less than his taking on and surviving the outraged onslaught of the most powerful governments in the world. The surprising fact of all this is that the Pakistan Government has refused the request for deportation, making a surprisingly tart reference to the West's dominance of international banking practices, and the consequent lack of the necessity for a nation outside the cartel to accede to such demands. No doubt Pakistan's reaction would have been more measured had she been physically smaller, and geographically placed between Colombia and Costa Rica. Then an operation entitled Credit Squeeze might well have been mounted, with the intention of bringing Mr Abedi back in handcuffs. As it is, the implications of this refusal are indicative of the fact that the self-righteousness of the West plays on an exposed nerve, and that there is, in many quarters of the globe, an unconcealed glee when the so-called G-7 nations are diddled by methods which they thought of as their own.

That a person from the underprivileged world should be responsible for the greatest fraud in the history of banking is in itself an almost incredible achievement in the eyes of many, and worthy of unqualified support. Every small boy in 80 per cent of the world's population will dream of being a Robin Hood, beating the ageing oracles of the West at their own games, and leaving science fiction and all that jazz to the spoiled scions of the other 20 per cent.

9 August 1991

In Praise of Laziness

The probing laser-beam of scientific research has succeeded in casting light on various obscure regions of human nature, while inevitably rendering the surrounding darkness darker still. 'Studies have shown . . .' the sentence invariably begins, and goes on to bring to our attention the findings of learned bodies, locked in the isolation of remote campuses, who have succeeded in coming to conclusions of undeniable value to an understanding of ourselves, and of nature, in which we are but infinitesimal organisms.

We have not yet reached the phase in which the supremos of science can warn us that breathing is bad for the health, or at least that starvation implies certain risks, but we know for a fact that each individual only exploits a minimal portion of the brain's potential. This finding suggests that the true key to life's adventure is the unlocking of the floodgate of knowledge which is every person's birthright, only just out of reach. All sorts of proverbs about idle hands, and biblical saws encouraging industry as the ideal ambiance for the practice of godliness, place us all on the straight and narrow. This gives the mind no time to consider temptation, which is, after all, one of the charms of existence.

Now come a welter of new findings by American researchers, in some measure contradicting the old ones. This is, of course, in the nature of things. There is absolutely no point in findings if they do not cast doubts on previous findings, thereby giving the individual the democratic right of choice. These new findings are the result of a technique called Time Budget Analysis,

7

or, one supposes, TBA. Whatever shortages exist in this ageing planet, a shortage of initials is not one of them.

What have the perpetrators of TBA discovered? Quite simply that the tireless beaver, the overworked ant, and the workaholic bee are, in fact, prime examples of indolence. These seeming examples of unity of purpose are, in fact, wayward creatures, the beaver only really seeming to work while being watched by humans with binoculars, but unable to match the stamina of humans in the art of total immobility, and therefore giving up the pretence of hard labour while still being watched, hence the findings. Bees quickly lose interest in the daily grind of pollinating flowers, and are easily deflected by jam left in spoons, and other substitutes.

As for ants, I have had occasion to watch them through the mosquito netting of an upper window in my house. One branch of a creeper leans rather negligently on the netting, much like a curl on a forehead. There is an endless procession of ants up and down the branch for no discernible purpose. They get to the mosquito netting, turn round and belt down again. One or two venture on to the netting itself, discover it to be impenetrable and inedible, rest awhile, and then, reinvigorated, rush down again, knocking those still climbing out of their way. The trouble with my kind of amateur research is that I have no means of identifying individual ants, and have therefore no way of knowing if the ants are all different ones, or whether they are the same ones going through the same motions time and again.

If they are, in fact, different, then the word that there is nothing worth having on the mosquito net does not get around very quickly. If, on the other hand, the ants are always the same ones, they may be playing some game unknown to us. The branch may be their Cresta Run, or giant slalom. If not, I regret to say that, despite their reputation for being highly evolved, they are just stupid. After all, we are highly evolved also.

TBA, with learned contributions from the Universities of Vermont, Ithaca. Minnesota, California, Illinois and Michigan, has proved conclusively, until the next findings at least, that most of the time our partners in this world, the animals, insects and birds, spend the largest part of their working hours doing absolutely nothing. Or at least, the minimum for the instinctive needs of survival, procreation, and other details. All this is easy to believe of oysters, for instance, which seem to spend their whole sad lives waiting for something to happen, and then, when it does, probably have a moment to wish it hadn't.

But I look back astounded at memories of the film *Quo Vadis*, and realize that oysters are not the only creatures drawn towards either an inherent or an acquired taste for immobility. On the hottest day this century, the lions were supposed to devour the Christians in the Colosseum. I remember every detail of this, since as Nero, I had the best seat in the arena. I gave the thumbs-down signal for the games to begin. There was a roar from the crowd as the lions ambled into the violent sunshine of the stadium. A few seconds later, they formed a queue to return to the sepulchral shade of their cages, and even the fact that they had not eaten for a couple of days did nothing to help them direct a few somnolent paces towards the crucified Christians, who were in fact dolls packed with raw meat. There we have it, a flagrant example of TBA at work.

It follows from all this that the natural state for both humans and others is asleep, or at least day dreaming. Anyone who enjoys work is understood to be either immensely ambitious, or else a flaunter of that brotherhood beloved of trades unions. The working day is growing shorter, and the weekend longer.

In Holland, a country always in the vanguard of permissiveness, it is now possible to evolve 'over-spanning' as a reason for going sick, and every worker has a right to diagnose himself, and, if he has the energy for it, sign the medical certificate. 'Over-spanning' means over-stressed, a victim of tension. Doctors no longer bother to diagnose a condition of which the patient is a better judge, and employers assume, if not 'over-spanned' themselves, that quite a few of their employees will be off at any given time. It has been known, although infrequently, for workers to be absent and over-spanned for a year or more on full pay.

Laziness comes as naturally to mankind as it does to the animal kingdom, on condition that the instincts are not tampered with by the mumbo-jumbo of lofty ethical considerations. To paraphrase the late Harry Truman, one lion might well say to another: 'If you can't stand the heat, stay out of the arena.' And the other lion, or lioness, might well reply: 'Shut up, and go to sleep.'

16 August, 1991

9

Beware of the Yoghurt Gangs

It is perhaps the conventional thing to do but we thought it only right to spend a few days in the south of France as in times gone by. Inevitably, I remember what the journey used to be like, either trying to sleep in the train, head wobbling to the rhythm of the ineptly named sleepers, or else driving down on the narrow roads which gave you many alternative routes to the sun with an exasperation quite different from that on the tedious autoroutes of today. Once there, there was room to park despite the milling crowds. There were just fewer cars, and those there were were less accessible to the many. In that sense, the joys of the seaside are more egalitarian and the fragments of pleasure and of horror more equally distributed. In those far-off days, only the affluent needed a parking place; today everyone needs one, and only a small fraction procure them. It is no longer a question of wealth or influence, but of luck, and often of chicanery.

We settle on an exorbitant mattress on the beach and read the morning paper to keep in touch with that world we have temporarily left behind. We are very self-consciously, on holiday. Only on holiday would you pay that price for a mattress. Holidays are different. And what do we read in our haven of peace and contemplation? Gangs of hooligans have been robbing the night trains from Paris. Gangs of burglars are systematically stealing valuables from jewellery shops and unisex hairdressers. Gangs of Peruvians are attacking and sometimes killing motorists on the highways leading from France into Spain. Some 120 Turks have crossed the border from Italy with the help of the Mafia and have gone into action, attacking people and selling hashish. There are so many miscreants actively at work that one has the uncanny feeling that not only the police, but even the population, will soon be outnumbered. In a way, such a glut of criminals, whom one can describe as belonging to liberal professions, takes the heat off the government in these days of rising unemployment. It is patently unnecessary to create jobs for people who are so expert at creating their own. But that is only the sparse silver lining of the darkest of clouds.

From the languages one hears spoken, screamed or shouted by our neighbours on the beach, the place is overflowing with those waiting with the patience of the very sick to go home once a change of regime allows it, and those who could go home now but find it more congenial on a foreign beach than to face the imponderable of life wherever they came from. You will have guessed perhaps that the prevalent vogue is for Arabic, followed only a touch more discreetly by Iranian. Close your eyes as you bake in the sun, and you could easily believe yourself to be in the Gulf, with only the shifting odour of tanning emulsions to replace the acid fumes of burning oil wells. Open your eyes and you see serried ranks of those dreaming of wider expanses of sand than at the moment at their disposal; only punctuated by little groups of distinguished Iranians, discreetly yelling their opinions of the assassination of Mr Bakhtiar. (I do not speak Iranian, but every third word is in French and every fourth one in English. Every fifth word is Bakhtiar). Interspersing this sea of anguished or melancholy humanity are isolated Italians, Germans, British and others keeping their own counsel in a kind of tense isolation: and small children of all ethnic traditions present, breaking down the barriers as only they know how, by playing together, by out-yelling each other, by throwing objects at each other which usually hit dozing adults, and by indulging in acts of war within the means at their disposal.

Eventually, driven into the water by the continuous turmoil on land, one loses sight of one's feet after a couple of steps in the swirling murk of disturbed sand. In clearer water, one usually encounters shoals of tiny fish, which dart hither and thither like flights of arrows. But in the gloom which pervades even the shallows, there is no sign of marine life other than floating bits of dishevelled seaweed. These were soon joined by a lady's powder puff which could easily have been taken for a rare type of sea anemone if it were not for the tag which said 'made in

Korea'. Other fragments of charred or soiled paper bobbed by, and I promptly stopped swimming with my mouth open. The climax to this maritime adventure was reached when I felt I was being followed. Turning discreetly. I noticed an immense condom which subsequently tried to attach itself to me as a stray dog will to a passer-by who seems remotely sympathetic. Wherever I swam, the condom seemed to follow. Just as in the kind of films it is the fashion to show after midnight on television, guaranteeing nightmares, the *tenue* of the tame condom was abruptly compounded by its appearance ahead of me. Had it overtaken me while I was attempting to do the crawl? No, I only had to wait for the condom to catch up with me to realize that there were now two of them. They were multiplying! I made my escape in the gap between them while there was still only two of them, and re-entered the chaos of the beach with a sense of relief, a sense of civilization rediscovered.

Under our balcony at the hotel there is a bar which announces proudly it is open all night — like the window of our room. Before retiring, we filled in the breakfast order: two grapefruit juices, coffee for two, toast and a couple of yogurts for 8am. We hung it on the handle of our door. South American rhythms, and the noise of joyless revelry continued until 6am. Some inebriated Scandinavians were singing in what was intended to be unison. There was a knock on our door. I opened it to two waiters pushing two tables on which were displayed seven grapefruit juices, two omelettes, four plates of cereal, five yoghurts, a mass of jams and cheeses and several pots of coffee. I said that it was not for us. The senior waiter showed me the breakfast order in my name, with a forged signature. and a huge and very flattering VIP scrawled all over the page. It said 6am. Apparently, there are gangs of middle-aged adolescents who amuse themselves by altering the breakfast orders, changing shoes left out for cleaning, and so on. Since they are never at hand to see the results of the confusion they create, I don't understand the joy it can bring them. I told Room Service that I would not need seven grapefruit juices in the future since I was travelling without my wives. Meanwhile, we are contemplating a return to our empty home, on holiday at last.

23 August, 1991

Season of Mists and Violence

The autumn season has begun despite the stubborn summer weather in most parts of the northern World. Rain threatens occasionally, a few drops fall, and then the smile of nature breaks through all barriers. One wonders what violence winter holds as a revenge for all this unseasonal clemency. Most people have a built-in sense of balance, a feeling for the accountancy of the environment, and while they enjoy what look like errors in celestial judgments, they also wonder about the price that they will have to pay when the mistake is discovered, and urgently rectified. How then do I know that autumn is here? Simply, because the calendar dictates that the months of idleness are over, and there is no future in attempting to recuperate for exertions yet to come.

Three days ago I was in Gothenburg, Sweden, in an atmosphere both cool and functional with a condiment of romantic idealism on the side. The reason I was there? A television appearance with a top Scandinavian entertainer, a musician and wit called Eddie Skoller. The audience was composed of local people who all seemed not only to understand English but to savour what I hope were finer points, and their laughter was amazingly identical to that in England, with subtle reactions to observations to which I never hoped for an audible signal of appreciation.

Walking through the streets, one is very conscious of the relaxed atmosphere of a functioning democracy, now imperceptibly recuperating from an indecisive election. Here there was no fear of the untidiness of a multi-party system as there always seems to be in England, where the freedom to govern in peace often supplements the need for more shades of opinion to be represented. As democracies go, the Swedish example is truer to its ideals than either of its British or American counterparts, and one cannot but be impressed as one strolls down broad and quiet streets, as underpopulated as the nation itself, that this part of the world is responsible for by far the highest per-capita contribution to international charity. There is an inherent civic sense in these parts, which is perhaps the consolation for its relative isolation and emptiness, but which is no less impressive for that.

On the television, weeping Croatians dominate the news. A brief stopover in Copenhagen, a touch-down in Birmingham, and a night in that outpost of originality and poetry, Dublin. Four countries between breakfast and tea. Walking in Dublin is full of surprises, such as four musicians in dinner jackets playing Vivaldi in Grafton Street, and the choreographic delights of a plastered tramp. Even the rain, while unseasonably wet, seems to be composed of grace notes tumbling in profusion.

Nevertheless, weeping civilians in Croatia have pride of place on the evening news. The next day an early start for Geneva, and an evening on the stage of the opera, not singing you'll be relieved to know, but reading selected texts by Voltaire to celebrate the end of a congress of international lawyers. Frederic Dard, the French crime author, and Prince Sadruddin Aga Khan read works by Calvin and Jean-Jacques Rousseau. The first part of the evening was serious, the second part an ebullient and sarcastic revue; Swiss lawyers laughing at themselves. A paradox? Never forget that Switzerland has produced not only bank managers but also some of the greatest clowns in the world, including Grock. Presumably since clowning requires a discipline and a vigour at least commensurate with that of a financier, this is merely the other side of the same coin, in this case a Swiss franc. Switzerland is yet again a small country with her eloquent message to the nascent European federation. She is more united by the historical facts of her own geography than she is separated by the differences in her four languages. The fact that she is the home of the most rigid conformity and also of its distorting-mirror image, the absurd Surrealism of logic pushed to the point of the illogical, is by no means an anomaly. It is Switzerland's invaluable contribution to the European condition.

Now, Pittsburgh. It is eight o'clock in the morning in Europe, not here. Here it is 2am, and I am writing my piece for *The*

European. The television is on to help me concentrate. Sometimes it puts me to sleep as nothing else will. The last thing I remember, very early this morning, on Swiss television was the weeping Croatians. However often the landscape and the habits of people change, the World of today recognizes what is important at any given time. Only on television here, the tragedy in Yugoslavia takes its place among other events, usually of local importance such as the outcome of ball games and the sordid contributions of witnesses to the latest murder. We are back in a big country with a heartbeat which is practically audible after all the different manifestations of smallness.

A meeting of the Democratic National Congress is in progress on one of the public service channels, and I try not to listen. Before shutting my ears to it, I have gathered, however, that it is a dinner of Democratic hopefuls to oppose George Bush at the next election. The first speaker, Mr Brown, the ex-Governor of California, said little to deflect attention from my work.

The second hopeful, a young fellow by the name of Dave McCurdy, grabbed my attention by stating in fiery tones that America is the oldest democracy in the world, and therefore worthy of respect. He was obviously expecting applause, and when none was forthcoming, he left a pause where it should have been. Then, describing himself as obvious presidential material, he allowed his voice to break when he told us that Dad and Mom had been married 49 years and a few months when the former passed away. A flyweight I dread hearing from again, if only as a worthy opponent to Dan Quayle. After this orgy of mediocrity, Jesse Jackson, confirming an opinion that he is far too lucid and intelligent an orator ever to hold high office.

My attention was diverted only once more before I finished my article. A woman who had the wild and silent look of someone who has absorbed more than her ration of abuse sat staring at nothing, while the female moderator of whatever programme it was said, 'Thank you for having shared your hostility with us'. You can say that again Lady. Any time. Any time.

27 September, 1991

16

On Sex, Sin and Stupidity

The last thing I want is to prolong a situation which has already made a miserable impact on British life and brought all the sainted holier-than-thou-brigade out of the woodwork. I refer to what would be a non event in most other countries, the questioning of the Director of Public Prosecutions while allegedly chatting to a prostitute in the King's Cross area of London. The fact that the eminent lawyer resigned as soon as his name had been taken by the zealous policemen suggests that the conversation was not about the adherence of Britain to the Common Market. It suggests it, but nothing is proven.

It is quite usual for the ladies of the night, and even the ladies of the late afternoon, to ply their trade in the vicinity of railway stations. This is a fact in many countries with large agglomerations of population and the consequent mass of commuters. Emerging from the station in Germany I began walking towards my hotel, which was so close that it did not warrant a taxi. Passing close to a prostitute I evidently surprised her by my presence in that particular city to the extent of her calling out 'Ach Mister Unicef!'

I had just appeared on German television in my capacity as ambassador for that organization, and this was such a charming slip of the tongue that I stopped to speak to the lady. It would have been churlish not to take the trouble. She was obviously a person who had known better times, and who performed her present job efficiently but without undue enthusiasm. She had a child to support and declared herself moved by the millions of children in less fortunate positions than her own daughter.

Because of this she gave money to Unicef whenever she could afford it. Now if Germany had the same kind of ill-conceived law as Britain, I might easily have been forced into declaring my identity to a roving policeman whose devotion to duty exceeded his humanity.

How would it have sounded to such a functionary if I had protested that I had been discussing Unicef? What, with a tart? And had the lady confirmed that we were talking about the state of the world's children, the whole encounter would have suggested a clumsy conspiracy to protect my name. On another occasion on the Austrian-German border I gave my passport to the Frontier guard. He glimpsed my photograph, shot me a look of alarm and yelled in a strident voice reminiscent of the unlamented gauleiters of the past: 'I'm holding on to this passport. Park your car in that space and come into the Customs shed.' I parked the car and got out shaking with anger. His attitude had changed completely in no time. He offered me my passport, his face wreathed in somewhat strenuous smiles. 'Gute reise,' he said. 'Good journey.' I asked him about the shouting earlier. He brushed it aside as a momentary lapse. I studied his face penetratingly. 'That's not true,' I ventured, 'you took me for a terrorist or something of the sort didn't you?' He explained his predicament with a little click of irritation. 'Every day before duty we are compelled to glance through photographic files of known terrorists still at large to refresh our memories.' It was his turn to look at me penetratingly. 'I knew that I had seen you somewhere before,' he said.

Only the other day, in England, I was stopped at 1.30am by a police patrol car in the tortuous centre of a small cathedral city. I was at the wheel of a rental car, driving slowly up the correct side of the road. The blue lights switched on behind me, stabbing the night with their accusing fingers. I didn't stop at once, since I could not imagine what I had done wrong. Then I understood that he could hardly use his siren at that hour in the morning in this residential environment. I stopped. The policemen came over and made peremptory gestures for me to lower my window.

Being a rented car, I did not immediately know how, which seemed suspect in this day and age. When at last I succeeded, I was told that my front and rear fog lights were on. I gazed at the dashboard which looked like that of one of the larger

Boeings, and wondered which pilot lights controlled the fog lights. Their suspicion of my comportment grew, until one of them recognized me, and asked me about the theatre and my professional life. I almost offered them a couple of complimentaries, but decided that that might look like bribery. They behaved with exquisite courtesy, and eventually, realizing that I was lost, escorted me 24km to my hotel.

I mentioned these anecdotes to illustrate the arbitrary nature of our relations with the law in these highly-strung days. In the case of the DPP, it is certainly the letter of the law at work, and not the spirit of justice. The tabloids refrained from emulating the Belgrano incident, by using the headline, 'Got 'im'. For that is what it was — a piece of atrocious luck. It never got as far as a moral issue. Used in this way, the police in the case are no better than sordid *agents-provocateurs*. To allow a splendid career to be ruined in such a way is neither tragic nor just. It is, alas, too plain stupid for that.

11 October, 1991

The Stuff Nazis are Made of

Don't be surprised if today's column is full of blanks, or at least allusions. I wish to cause no pain, except where it is deserved. I name no names and quote no numbers. They are already reported to the proper authorities: the hotel in which I was staying, which included a witness to this incident from the outside. The reason for the blanks is that I wish to spare the reader the full blast of the obscenities which were shouted and which are, in any case, unprintable.

The scene was a modern, commercial hotel in the north of England. I ordered a taxi to go to a Chinese restaurant of high local repute. After a short while, the taxi arrived. I squeezed in and took no particular note of the driver, except to register that he was white-haired and fairly massive. He did not react when I told him the address of our destination. I assumed that he was a strong, silent type. He looked right to see if there was any oncoming traffic, but failed to look forward before accelerating. Had he done so, as I did out of force of habit, he would have noticed a black gentleman crossing our bows on foot.

This gentleman, who seemed in the dark to be dressed in a track-suit, had every reason to believe that he had been observed by my driver. He had not been, and contact was made. It was only owing to the extreme nimbleness and lightning reaction of the pedestrian that a drama was averted. I dread to think what would have happened had the pedestrian been old.

Naturally the driver jammed on the brakes. Both men must have suffered unpleasant shocks. The black gentleman was the first to recover, and brought his fist down three times on the taxi's bonnet, shouting out his fury at the driver's negligence. This touched a nerve in my strong silent type, who let go a string of expletives, alluding to the man's colour with a pungency and subtlety of a kind I had not heard since leaving the army.

Conditioned reflexes took over and the near-victim danced over to the driver's side of the car, and attempted to punch him with a series of straight rights. The driver accelerated away, regardless of any traffic, and suddenly braked. He turned, wide-eyed with rage, his face expressing nothing but sheer hatred and urgency, and he attempted to run down the black gentleman with the rear of his cab. I shouted at close quarters. His eye caught mine. Our faces were only a few inches apart. He seemed to come to what senses he possessed. The rest of our miserable journey, during which he let his pent-up fury be reflected in the sheer chaos of his driving skills, was a litany of scurrilous vulgarities at the expense of the black community, laced with admonitions to them to return to their virgin forests. He must have assumed that I was foreign, since I didn't speak with the warm local burr. 'D'you 'ave trooble with the niggers where you coom from?' he asked, or rather yelled, as we arrived. 'We don't even have trouble with our whites,' I said, but it was too much to expect him to understand something so fragile as a nuance. He was hermetically sealed against any viewpoint other than his own. As I paid him, I told him with all the calm objectivity I could muster that he was responsible for the incident. He woke up to what I had said.

'Is that so?' he bellowed, seeming to wish to get out. I told him he ought to be bloody well ashamed of himself, and added that I was sure he drove more carefully when alone in the cab than when he had passengers. I was wrong. He accelerated away with a squeal of tyres, looking back at me with sheer loathing. Luckily, this time there was no one in the way.

Naturally, we have all come across intolerance in some form or other, be it the quietly taunting southern sheriff, so often brilliantly observed by actors on the screen, or the depressing interview with incredibly obtuse South African right-wingers on television, or yet encounters in life which alarm and strain at credulity. I must confess that I have never before experienced at such close quarters the very stuff of which Nazis are made; the militancy of loneliness, the search for a communal belief since the mind is too muddled and inadequate to give credence to any personality of one's own; the comfort of a shared footfall in march rhythm, the sentiment of belonging which fills the otherwise cringing brain with the illusory courage of a common cause, even an immoral one.

There is desperation at the root of all this — even panic. And of course, massive doses of cowardice, the inability to look the world in the eye, or facts in the face. It is horrible and pathetic at the same time.

As with a snake-bite, one looks around hurriedly for the antidote. It was not long in coming. Another taxi was called to take me home. I said before its arrival that if the driver turned out to be the same fellow by some mischance, I would not take it.

This driver was even larger than the first, too large in fact to look back except in the mirror. I consequently never saw his face in its entirety, only the unruly mass of grey curls which covered his huge head and fell round the top of his collar like an ornament. There seemed to be not much neck. His voice was soft and measured, full of confidence, but at no times more than that. I told him the whole wretched story of my earlier experience. He expressed no particular surprise.

'I'll tell you what,' he said. 'There will be no charge for this cab. I don't want you thinking ill of this city.' I waved as he drove off. He gave me the thumbs-up sign.

18 October, 1991

Devious Paths to Freedom

Ivan likes to describe himself as an average Russian, whatever that is. He has a snub nose and wide-set, small eyes which seem to be brown until he comes close to you, when they turn out to be blue. His manner is diffident, since he feels a little out of his depth in the West, and does not wish his ignorance of the ways of free democracies to show too outrageously. In fact, he has been sent, like so many others, on a fact-finding tour. His trip has unfortunately served to confuse him even further. He confessed himself to me.

'Piotr lonovich,' he said, 'I was well looked after in America. They evidently felt they had an almost religious duty to instruct me in the devious ways of freedom. They realize, as I do, that there is no use in having freedom if you don't know what to do with it, and so they gave me what they called "guidelines" for the exercise of freedom.'

'Guidelines?' I inquired.

'Yes. They explained to me that I had rights, which came as a great relief to me, as you can imagine. They then explained further that everyone else had rights as well, to the extent that it gives individuals practically no room for manoeuvre.'

'Oh, you must have misunderstood.'

'I don't think so. While I was under instruction, the case of Judge Thomas was unfolded on television, preventing my coming to terms with my jet lag. It seemed to contradict many of the things I had been so piously told.'

'Such as?'

'Why is the length of his organ a criterion in judging his ability to be wise?'

'No. You have seized on the least edifying aspect of the inquiry.'

'As an ex-artillery officer I can tell you that length by itself is irrelevant unless it is taken in conjunction with diameter,' he insisted.

'All that is incidental,' I counter-insisted. 'It was the claim of a former assistant of his that he had boasted of his physical fortune while in the course of harassing her sexually. It has absolutely no bearing on his quality as a judge.'

'But was he being assessed as a man or as a judge?'

'Both.'

'Both? Impossible. If you insist on equating the private man with the public figure, you are asking for trouble.'

'How do you do it back home?'

'I don't know. But I know how we used to do it. Behind closed doors. The choice of a judge was the business of the Party and the Central Committee, and that was that. Few people even knew his name, let alone his physical propensities. And as for harassment, there were very few women worth harassing.' He sighed. 'Now that they are all under the influence of Pierre Cardin and Yves Saint Laurent, I suppose all that will change. Men will find beauty where they least expect it, at work.'

'How would you translate harassment into Russian?' I asked.

He smiled. 'As you can imagine, there are many words, although none of them is really accurate. What is needed is a subtle word expressing more than invitation and less than rape, which is, at the same time, the opposite of courtship. There is as yet no provision for such a word in our language. It will have to be invented if we are further to submit to the influence of the West.'

'The opposite of courtship?' I asked, puzzled.

'Yes. If a proposal of marriage is accepted, the process which led up to the proposal is called courtship. If it is refused, it is called harassment. The process is identical.' I decided not to pursue the subject any further. He seemed to be musing on some great truth or other which was troubling him. 'It seems to me,' he said at length, 'that the Americans try to leave nothing to chance, at the same time paying lip service to liberty, which is by its very nature a vote of confidence in chance. While they are experiencing the height of embarrassment in the investigation of Judge Thomas, a man walks into a supermarket and kills twenty-three people, including himself. Guns are allowed to be used in self-defence. What happened in the supermarket seems to me to be carrying self-defence too far.'

'In any case,' I said, 'the part of the constitution which allowed personal weapons was intended for flintlock pistols, not for Rambo rejects in army surplus stores. Life changes, with the law struggling to catch up in the background.'

'It is the same everywhere,' he said, seeming to see daylight. 'I don't think there is as much difference between our systems as everyone makes out, except that in our country reputations were protected by secrecy, and in America they are open to scrutiny.'

'That is all the difference in the world,' I suggested.

'It's the difference between a one-party system and a two-party system where there is no real difference between the parties,' he replied. 'With us, all was secret. With them, it is a sport. American politics resembles the Super Bowl. And it even affects areas where politics should play no part, like the selection of judges.'

'And Britain in all this?' I asked, eager to remain within my depth.

'The most mysterious of both worlds,' he said in a hushed voice. 'I reached there just as the television franchises were being handed out. Can you explain to me the logic of the decisions?'

'No,' I replied frankly.

'Central Television knew that it had no rival in its area, bid £2000, and won its franchise. Others put up millions of pounds and lost to those offering less. Who decides such things. It can't be the market.'

'A commission,' I said.

He was alarmed. 'A commission or a committee?' he asked.

'The great change was at the instigation of Margaret Thatcher,' I tried to explain. 'She was incensed by a programme from Thames TV about the killing of an IRA group in Gibraltar. She called it Trial by Television.'

'Thames TV's franchise was not renewed,' he said sharply. 'Nor was TV-am, but here she wrote a mea culpa to its chief executive.'

'How do you know all this?' I asked.

'It's all part of my report,' he replied. 'This seems like one of democracy's many malfunctions.'

'I don't think it has much to do with democracy.' I muttered, 'unless you believe that without Emile Zola, Captain Dreyfus would have died on Devil's Island, and without television Senator McCarthy would have finalized his havoc, and the Irish would still be languishing in English jails. Yes, of course, it has everything to do with democracy! Bravo, Ivan.'

25 October, 1991

Of Paragons and Parasites

Human nature, as we all know, is by no means perfect. It has many sides, many aspirations — the rare triumphs, the immense range of shortcomings. The first efforts at purifying the spirit came with the birth of organized religion and the mystification of simple faith into secret rituals, involving vestal virgins, oracles and the like. With progress came the monasteries and the nunneries, each group in its own way seeking to wash the soul clean by various abstinences, imposing mortification of the flesh or voluntary degradation of the human condition by vows of silence and other even colder comforts.

At times, man takes these initiatives himself, or else provokes situations in which such trials become inevitable. After five long years, Terry Waite emerged from a terrible isolation which, while not self-imposed, was at least invited. His name was kept alive during his disappearance by the memory of his mission, his dedication to the Church of England and a sentiment that here was a man somewhat out of the ordinary. This was confirmed at the moment of his release. Brushing aside those who wished to protect him against the shock of the first contact with the outside world after the chained solitude of his darkened cell, he spoke like a trained communicator, tersely, economically, with a kind of tough restraint, unwilling to condemn his captors outright, displaying the Christian virtue of humility as a kind of indomitable secret weapon. It even, ultimately, caused his captors to apologize for having kept him incommunicado for more than five years, and to admit that it had served no useful purpose.

There must be many who admire his steadfast faith without

pretending to share it — but there can be few who were not deeply moved and profoundly impressed by his performance.

Very soon afterwards, another sort of pioneer plumbed the depths of his human resources to surpass himself in a more secular field of endeavour. Gerard d'Aboville rowed single-handed across the Pacific, a feat which seems almost inconceivable to one who, even in his heyday, found it impossible to row across the Serpentine in London's Hyde Park. Once again, if for a fundamentally different reason, man was pitted against the seeming infinity of loneliness. Here was the rage of the elements instead of the enforced immobility in a bleak cell. Thirty-six times, or it may have been thirty-eight (the haggard mariner no longer remembers), the boat capsized and had to be righted again in mountainous seas. And yet, after all that, the speck of dust on limitless horizons arrived in a safe harbour. The navigator took off his woollen headgear to reveal a balding head, and huddled with his family, as in a miniature rugby scrum, so that their tears of relief mingled on their faces.

No one can ever succeed in tarnishing their achievements while their solitude lasted. They were unobserved, and emerged as evidence of what man is capable if endowed with a special sense of daring.

Now, of course, they have rejoined the human race, the daily grind of life in contact with others of the species, and immediately, before we have time to meditate on their achievements, they are sullied by those ever-present elements of jealousy which accompany every odyssey like a flight of screeching gulls. Terry Waite, we learn, had only himself to blame for being captured. He was always a man of undeniable arrogance, we hear from those who remember him from long ago. He was doctrinaire, others add, and pompous and opinionated. And what was his relationship with Oliver North, the Iranians, weapons in general? The terriers of investigative journalism bark self-righteously until all the many versions of the truth are revealed and are indistinguishable from each other.

But surely someone who merely rows thousands of miles cannot be subjected to the same innuendos as a man who sets out bravely, or in a spirit of foolhardiness, to rescue some hostages? There can be no hidden strings attached to the one, even if the other could conceivably have had connections with politicians or security services? Don't you believe it. No sooner had the rowing boat safely docked than there were immediate allegations that the near shipwrecks had been engineered for publicity purposes, with the aim of personal aggrandizement.

Where do such rumours spring from, if not from the devious minds of those who cannot take initiatives by temperament, but can only live, like parasites, on the initiatives of others? Unable to enter the minds of those unafraid of being alone, and therefore bereft of the secrets of personal security, they live in groups, for ever in search of willing ears. And with the ever faster and more efficient communications between the ends of the earth, these are not hard to come by.

It does not matter that the idea of a man deliberately capsizing his boat between thirty and forty times in an icy sea in order to seek publicity strikes one as particularly asinine. Nor does it matter that Terry Waite's statement on his liberation hardly seemed to be the words of one with a great deal to hide.

There will always be mud that clings doggedly to their brilliant achievements. Why? Because we who hear the words of suspicion or calumny are also members of the same human race, always open to most suggestions, titillated by unexpected whispers, secretly eager for evident verities to be proved false. Life holds no greater interest for some of us than this. And this despite the fact that there are sufficient buffoons around to satisfy all our predilection for malice without having to tarnish images too dazzling for our comfort.

Take the outrageous events in Yugoslavia, for instance, now that the peace initiatives are well on the way to being as frequent as the disasters to Monsieur d'Aboville's boat. The face of Lord Carrington, frozen into a mask of disenchantment, and the whimsical expression of Cyrus Vance can do little to reassure us, while the stiff demeanour of Mr Tudjman and the sly smile of Mr Milosevic appear, in stark contrast to the real suffering of real people, the most eloquent and unanswerable form of investigative journalism.

29 November, 1991

Out of Bleak Clouds, Hope

As 1992 begins, we are catching up on a year of insomnia and jet-lag in the most prestigious hotel suite in the world, the so-called Joseph Conrad Suite at the Oriental Hotel, Bangkok. It is an oasis within an oasis: a supremely mellow retreat with four-poster beds, high ceilings and a view over luxuriant gardens and the bustling Phao Chya river, with its characteristic Thai long-boats, powered by the noisiest of outboards and driven by pro-pellers at the end of the longest of poles.

It is not the sheer luxury of the Joseph Conrad Suite which is awe-inspiring, but the discreet patina of history which has given it an indefinable cachet. The great man lived in this room when it was still No. 1 in the original hotel. Now that the hotel has grown in size, the towering annexes dwarf the old building, and No. 1 has become No. 101 — a sign, one imagines, of progress.

Conrad himself was a Pole, belonging to a nation not famous for its seafarers, but who became the leading literary seafarer of a country with a long tradition of navigation. And only at the age of sixteen did he begin to tackle the English language.

This historical aura is exactly the kind in which I can comfortably cocoon myself for a short period of meditation: a period to be savoured moment by moment, like a fine wine. All good things must come to an end, they say — but that is not the right philosophy, unless one realizes that it is a miracle that the good things even started. The way that led to this oasis was a case in point.

The road between Bangkok's airport and the hotel is one of the saddest in my experience. Not because it bears evidence of human suffering, as do such highways in other Asian or African countries, but because it carries the hallmark of what is called prosperity: thousands of ultra-modern high-rises arbitrarily placed in a featureless modern landscape, and half-lost in the midst of pollution. These buildings are as rewarding of study as are a scattering of crumbs on a dirty tablecloth.

They reminded me of other high-rises in even more unexpected places — the little capitals of tiny African countries abandoned by Western powers when colonialism was no longer fashionable. Now they stand incongruously on the outskirts of what were only recently bloated villages: a mark of the First World's return in a new form after the elaborate farewells and lowering of flags a quarter of a century ago. Those addicted to prosperity believe sincerely that if they themselves are prosperous, the effect will be immediately beneficial on those less prosperous than themselves. This is the whole basis of conservative philosophy, and it may well be true, as far as it goes, under the ideal circumstances of perpetual growth (as elusive an ideal as perpetual motion).

But what happens in times of recession; times in which pundits continually read signs of levelling-off in the thunder clouds? Even those most cautious in their assessments believe they discern silver linings beginning to emerge as the darkness envelopes them. I, a greenhorn in financial matters, and with an often dangerously optimistic nature, confess to seeing nothing but an unrelieved and lugubrious fog around me — with no trace of so much as a *pewter* lining to the clouds, or the flicker of a match to illuminate the landscape.

And why should there be? Everywhere multinational companies are busy streamlining their operations by laying off thousands of employees, money for investment is scarce, and those coy and romantic people, the bankers, have been diddled out of trillions of dollars by a succession of international swindles which caused a loss of confidence in Confidence itself.

Meanwhile the East chooses freedom, at enormous cost. Rarely will good news have proved so prohibitively expensive.

It is the duty, a duty of self-preservation, for the West to assure as quickly and silently as possible the stability of its future partners in the East. And meanwhile the South gazes upon us with understandably baleful eyes. Is all the help it urgently needs being siphoned off to help the East?

When will it be paid prices for its raw materials that are no longer ludicrously disproportionate to the cost of manufactured goods which the South's nations have to import? Meanwhile, the South takes the only kind of revenge it can for the enforced impoverishment it suffers: sending an endless trail of immigrants to the prosperous and overcrowded West. This then sparks conflict, between the high ideal of offering open frontiers to refugees and the jealous defence of our own jobs in our own environment.

Are there saving graces to these pictures of gloom? Certainly. The situation is at least fluid. Anything can happen at any moment, and we must be ready for any eventuality at any time. It is, of course, disquieting for the Dick Cheneys of the world, who are always happier if they know where they stand. Rows of long-range missiles, and nuclear bombs airborne for 24 hours a day (like the better kind of room service) ironically make for a good night's sleep — whereas the present chaos causes ulcers.

And Boris Yeltsin, dealing with problems that have beset Russia since the days of Genghis Khan as though they were merely matters for peremptory decree, worries all professional administrators. The fact remains — perhaps as Yeltsin has discovered — that the only way to deal with gigantic problems is indeed not to be impressed by their size, and to deal with them as though they were negligible.

The situation is fluid, with all its dangers and with all its compensating hopes. Vast changes have been effected virtually without bloodshed for the first time in recorded history.

Rational thought is gaining ground at the expense of emotional claptrap, and even if religion is still a divisive force between nations, the need for a spiritual as well as a material life is becoming daily more evident.

Is there then room for hope, despite the gathering night? Neither hope nor confidence is in short supply. They have been in the past.

3 January, 1992

Cold War's Cosy Warmth

It is precisely a year since the Gulf War broke out. Many people believe it ended with commendable speed, thereby saving human life. Others may well reflect that it has not yet come to an end. Far from it. Naturally there have been changes as a result of the victory on the field of battle, some of them highly significant, others left incomplete and unresolved.

On reflection, there was one positive element in the Cold War, and that was simply that the two Superpowers had each other to worry about. Even if they specialized in terrifying noises and disturbing initiatives, such as the invasion of territories in their immediate neighbourhood, fitting the sinister description of zones of influence, on the whole they left the rest of us alone, so profoundly were they hypnotized by one another.

Now one side has opted out of the Cold War to be followed naturally by the other. What else was there to do? The result is that there is only one Superpower left, perhaps for the first time in global affairs. This may seem a unique advantage and yet it imposes its own pressures.

The Romans always had the Carthaginians and the Barbarians to breathe down their necks and *Terra Incognita* to contemplate. Later, when Spain and Portugal colonized South America by a technique which might be described as the carrot and the cross, the British and French were busy getting the northern third of the continent. At the dizziest heights of empire the British always had the French to contend with, and in Europe they both had to come to terms with the ambitions of a unified Germany.

There was always, by tradition, the other party. And consequently there was always a balance of power, constituted by uncommitted observers to the scene. Today there is no power to balance, and for the long distance runner in the race only loneliness to deal with. This is perhaps a contributory factor to the United States' eager espousal of the United Nations, not only as a catalyst for those forces in the world opposed to Saddam Hussein's unilateral actions, but also as a form in which cost-sharing could be freely discussed and confidentially negotiated.

For being a lonely leader has a host of new inconveniences at a time when the cost of sophisticated warfare has soared out of all proportion to the inflation rate, and when any military adventure has to be budgeted with the utmost vigour, especially if the conflict, as is so often the case, continues rather longer than expected.

With the actual fighting in the Gulf War quiescent and no other major war claiming the headlines, the world is full of weapons, most of them obsolescent, with which to lead the deprived into temptation.

One reads with amazement of Thailand purchasing large quantities of Chinese weapons at bargain prices, including more than 100 tanks, pontoon-laying trucks, armoured personnel carriers and 300 armoured cars. The Thai authorities had expected these weapons to be delivered with Western manufactured artillery, but to their surprise the guns were of Soviet manufacture so the shells were not interchangeable with those of the American tanks already owned by the Thai forces.

It seems astonishing in this increasingly technological age that such mistakes can still be made, or rather such details were left to chance. It reminds one of the theatre in Philadelphia where they clean forgot the need for dressing rooms, or the one or two examples of family dwellings in which the usefulness of toilets was entirely overlooked by the architects.

Naturally, the glut of armaments, even lying dormant, with matching ammunition or even without it, is a source of worry to those who have overnight assumed the mantle of solitary leadership. They lord it over a huge military industrial complex, to borrow one of General Eisenhower's few brilliantly coherent phrases, which now has suddenly no precise function, and a future with no great certainties apart from massive unemployment. This chaotic military landscape is complicated further by do-it-yourself efforts from various quarters at making rudimentary nuclear weapons or delivering the most hideous riches of biological warfare onto everybody's doorsteps.

Now that there is a prolonged pause in the Gulf war, United Nations teams are trying to assess exactly how advanced Iraq was in her acquisition of such sordid status symbols, with, for the moment, uncertain success. Obviously, if we had not embarked on this latter-day crusade, the armoury of secret weapons would still be intact, but had we finished the war as it should have been finished, it might have been an easier job to assess the past threat of Iraq by picking through the rubble unhindered in quest of evidence.

One thing is certain, sanctions would have had their effect even without a war, to judge by the parlous state of Iraqi children and the aged. But then, they would probably have suffered most in any case, in the light of priority accorded over there. To continue sanctions today is to carry the unended war into the ranks of future generations and those unable to defend themselves. Sanctions today are mean-minded and do little credit to the victors. It is not sanctions that will loosen Saddam Hussein's lean and efficient grip over the imaginations of his own people. The Achilles heel of our resolve is to be found elsewhere.

The solitary runner is leading the rest of the field by such a margin that, in his tender heart, he is chary of emphasising his advantages, lest he lose touch with the other runners altogether. War never looks so good in retrospect, when the errors of judgment and prevalent doubts begin to be uncovered by historians. And the prosecution of war is even more costly than its prevention.

The Cold War! Those were the restful days. At least you knew where you stood. There was always another runner in the corner of your eye.

24 January, 1992

35

The Old Bull and Bush

Viewed from Bangkok, we have the astonishing vision of George Bush charging over the landscape on a mission abroad touted as being entirely for internal consumption. While admittedly abroad, he seems to say, he has in reality never left the Oval office, since his mission is to persuade workers in paddy fields, among others, that a Cadillac is a sound investment for those in search of status, while there is always the Lincoln for the rugged individualist, or the Chrysler for the maverick. This sales pitch, he tells everyone including those up to their hips in rice, will create jobs in America, and therefore be good for the equilibrium of the planet.

Bush's most cogent arguments are reserved for the Japanese, of course, but once he is in the region it would be impolitic if not actually impolite to leave the paddy workers out of his calculations. Let's face it, with the cataclysmic collapse of the other competitor in the arms race, and with it the sudden realization that the long epoch of military confrontation has entered unlamented into history, America has been at pains to find a quick replacement on the more modern battleground of economics. Here, once a nation is not yet used to life without an enemy, or at least without a competitor, the obvious choice is Japan.

Historically, graced with such golden institutions as the Harvard Business School, America feels with some justification that she has a lot to teach others in the grasp of abstractions and global vision. As Calvin Coolidge said: 'The business of America is business,' and a proprietary note is struck in this phrase, a hint of exclusivity and even of ownership. In fact, America has gone so far along the road of sophistication that she sees herself as the first nation able to risk the hazards of total freedom, and to be able to turn it to her advantage. Certainly, her ideals remain doggedly and pristinely intact, however much the image is at times muddied by reality. Reality? Well, first of all total freedom doesn't exist in the world of the living, and secondly, if the business of America is indeed business, this suggests by its very nature a necessary degree of pragmatism, of rolling with the punches, of turning blind eyes, of politics.

And there, America can always boast with absolute assurance that she is more free than most, especially since we live in times in which it is fashionable to appear free. Japan is now a constitutional democracy which has paid the penalty of bitter defeat and humiliation by becoming a country of untold wealth and acumen. The same tragic events rendered the same service to Germany and both countries took the precaution of assuring the permanence of this state of affairs by writing into their new constitutions that their troops could never be used in service outside their own territories. This fact was greeted by their conquerors as proof of evolution and a change of heart. Until recently, that is, when the astuteness of these moves were brought home to the impoverished winners of that conflict. No nation, least of all the United States, can be goaded into a position of attempting to influence a thing as sacrosanct as a constitution, even if it is not its own. All it can do is to rattle the money boxes, as it did at the outbreak of the Gulf War, suggesting that the richest should make a contribution towards a war of the United Nations, a hint which was graciously taken in the interests of future harmony.

Italy, sadly, did not reap the same benefits as her erstwhile partners, since she came over to the Allied side in the conflict just a little too early. The morality of this is obvious, I believe.

The great and valid change which undeniably did take place was that our opponents in the last war, two dictatorships and one Celestial Empire, became democracies. In Germany's case, this change was carried out with characteristic thoroughness, so that Germany now possesses one of the most equitable, if most complicated, electoral systems in use today. Italy, more volatile by temperament, keeps her head above water by a series of dexterous combinations, creating numerous governments as ephemeral as zabaglione.

37

However, it is Japan which is the real worry to the earnest and analytical American mind, because there must be a lurking suspicion that despite the terrible loss of face occasioned by surrender and the peremptory rule of MacArthur, and despite enormous surface changes in obedience to altered values in the modern world, the ancient social structures and codes of behaviour are still in place, as mysterious and impenetrable as ever. The forthright and finally ingenuous American approach has no chance against so much which is unsaid, merely understood. To tell a geisha in the middle of a tea ceremony to take it easy is the kind of solicitude which is neither wanted nor appreciated.

Poor Mr Bush. He seems convinced that his frankness and entertainment value will finally be understood in the sea of smiles which surround him. He may well eke out a few concessions, so long as those are deemed cosmetic, not fundamental, by the donors.

'After all,' the Japanese seem to suggest, 'you have shown us that perfidy is punished, in the aftermath of Pearl Harbour. By the same token, should the virtues of hard work not be rewarded? Who are you to be our competitor and the umpire at the same time? Is it our duty to maintain your standard of living? Do quality and reliability in manufactured goods carry a penalty? If so, why?'

To be fair, there have been highly successful cases of collaboration between Japanese and American manufacturers. Mitsubishi and Chrysler had an agreement, and launched a successful small car on the market called a Colt. Eager to launch a sports car as a follow-up, the Mitsubishi executives decided on another equine name. The result was the Mitsubishi Starion, now on the market. The name was phoned through to Chrysler from Japan. What they had in mind was a Stallion, but it sounded different to the secretary in Detroit.

One wonders if Japanese journalists have been badgering John Major for the dates of the General Erection?

10 January, 1992

Ponderings in Paradise

Good news in paradise seems almost like too much of an indulgence. Paradise is here in any case, in the form of an isolated beach in Southern Thailand, with sand of an unadulterated purity and water of a consistently ideal temperature, through which you can discern every toenail individually. The whole is framed in flowers of such opulence that they are quickly taken for granted, and would only be noticed by their absence.

Naturally there are shortcomings, which only underline the proximity of all this to perfection; it could be that the French cheeses lack the serenity they enjoy back home and that the breakfast rolls are made with inferior local flour, an example of the effect of protectionism on the tastebuds, but these are tiny sacrifices which greed makes to the possibility of relaxing body and soul under ideal conditions, and must be borne with fortitude.

Now, into this apparently safe hermitage, a kind of isolation ward of the spirit, trickles the good news on one level, and the bad on the other. *The European* has been saved by two brothers who shun publicity because they wish not only to have a private life, but to enjoy it. Far be it from me to disobey these implicit instructions by drawing attention to them in an artless way, or even by mentioning their names yet again.

All I feel bound to do is to mutter a discreet word of gratitude as in a litany, and to reiterate my feelings of admiration for the skeleton staff of this paper, who have been battling with atrocious difficulties under trying climactic conditions while I have been floating on my back in a tepid sea, studying the sky for signs. All we had in common was our faith. This event was an inspiring example of enlightened capitalism, just as the previous life of this paper was an example of capitalism at its most dangerous, at its most capricious.

We hear, even in this remote part of this exquisite planet, that the brothers in question were not unimpressed by the devotion to an ideal demonstrated by the editor and his personnel, and that they had been readers of the paper they now own. In other words, conviction plays a part in this purchase, not merely a desire for acquisition. And other events never hesitate to underline the importance of conviction in human affairs. I mentioned the bad news which seeps through under the door, or even more on the discreet television screens of this island paradise. Mark you, the news to which I refer is not really bad, in the sense that unnecessary deaths in Yugoslavia or other examples of man's inhumanity to man are bad, if habitual. The news to which I draw attention is melancholy, and once again involves conviction and the lack of it. The reception of Mr Bush's precipitate rush through the Orient in search of pre-election jobs for derelict citizens in his great country has been greeted with intense embarrassment throughout the Far East. The excellent *Bangkok Post*, in its daily cartoon, even indulges in harsh derision. Depicted is a car crowded with avid American executives, with Bush at the wheel and Old Glory hanging limply from the aerial. On its coachwork is written, graffiti-wise, 'Japan or Bust', and further 'Buy American by Americans'. The car has lost all its wheels, three of which lie supine amid a mass of nuts and bolts which the car has shed, while in the middle-distance, the fourth wheel is still rolling away on its own, being bowed deeply to by two polite Japanese officials. The cartoon says it all with an unkindness which is as unusual in these climes as it is usual back home.

Miyazawa, the Japanese Prime Minister, suggested with his unflappable tact that we must all learn to understand the other's point of view, suggesting that he was doing what he could, but that his guests had not yet made much discernable effort in that direction. Admittedly, Mr Bush surpassed himself on the superficial level of public relations, playing the emperor at tennis and losing, and collapsing at an official dinner.

Although this provoked Barbara Bush into a wonderfully adroit and human reaction, it was no counterweight to the quarrelsome interviews of Detroit's top brass, who the president misguidedly invited to tag along on his team. Some might describe their contribution as forthright, others as clumsy.

The answer to their petulant demands for an open market lies in the cartoon. The scattering of working parts over the road suggests without undue subtlety that quality control is not of the best and that the concepts of Detroit, despite some cunning imitations of Japanese and European styling, are still fundamentally archaic, producing silent and stately boulevard vehicles for local conditions, often underpowered in the interests of economy.

It takes more than the protests of Detroit executives — in ever more strident voices — that they have become competitors to convince world opinion. The Orient may well have mysterious ways in which to close their markets to foreign intrusion, but how do you explain the colossal success of Japanese cars in the United States?

It is due basically to the fact that Japanese manufacturers have satisfied the desires of the American consumer, which the native product was unable to. Every respectable American motor magazine has been sounding this warning of things to come ever since Japan began to export cars. The Lexus and Infiniti were hailed as threats to Mercedes, BMW and Jaguar in the luxury car field.

There is another way to view freedom. In a free market in the USA, or in the allegedly unified one in Japan, it is equally difficult to force the consumer to buy goods he does not want. BMW is the most successful foreign import into Japan, but then BMW is a car produced out of conviction rather than consensus.

Finally, two opinions about the visit, both Japanese according to AP. One pessimistic: 'It was practically meaningless and only a loss for him.' The other optimistic: 'Japan felt that it had to help Bush. After all, he collapsed.'

17 January, 1992

When Mystery is Missing

How different the world must have looked when the words *Terra Incognita* still had a meaning full of beckoning menace, the Unknown World continually enticing potential merchants like Christopher Columbus and rendering hardened mariners like Juan de la Cosa nervous!

Characteristically, the Admiral Columbus always wished to sail a little further towards the thin line of the horizon, while de la Cosa, the captain, looked back fondly to where land had been so recently, his own. This fiction is a true reflection of the tendencies of society, the amateurs, politicians and captains of industry, always harking after the impossible, restrained by the professionals, the civil servants or the military, explaining firmly that it can't be done. Sometimes, in this conflict, the charisma of the amateur is such that no amount of clarity or logic deployed by the professionals is sufficient to break his wild initiative. Fortunately no one could influence the crazy desire of Christopher Columbus to find the Indies. Unfortunately there were no voices riveting enough to deflect Hitler, Napoleon, or Stalin from their policies.

Today, however, there is hardly a square inch of territory which can properly be described as incognita. Occasionally, an outsize footprint is discovered, either in the jungle of Malaysia or on the slopes of Everest, suggesting that there are still forms of life unknown to us; huge, shy creatures who have not yet reached the stage of evolution where a visit to the shoe department of the Big Man's Shop is imperative. Every clue of this sort is greeted with a little shudder of delight by a developed world, whose existence is quickly beginning to be short of mystery. And mystery is an element in life almost as important as oxygen.

We can feel this acute shortage by the great increase of those who escape from the rat race of daily existence by investing in small boats, in which to challenge the elements like toy replicas of the Great Columbus. For a day or more at a time, these battalions of latter-day explorers lose sight of land, although rarely of each other, in their effort to get away from it all. They sense, as they tug on the ropes, a vague thrill of uncertainty, of the unscripted, of a nature which might turn churlish at any moment. Certainly, the romantic amateurs, those who have pitted themselves against unequal forces, have a much greater following among those living humdrum existences than do the heads of department, the people with a foot on the brake pedal, whose mission it is to defend common sense against any trace of fantasy. It is only when the tiny adventure is at an end that the humdrum, the logical, takes over once again. The boats, those little plastic instruments for dreaming, are aligned in their marinas on numbered piers, like books on their shelves in a lending library.

Our need for mystery and what one might describe as dreaming space is underlined by the wild profusion of science-fiction films which, in their burning desire to break new ground, become neo-medieval, influenced by the antics of the Samurai and other crypto-Kung Fu phantasmagoria, and as such begin to be what was never intended: terribly alike. It is as though even our fantasies are signposted, every flight on schedule. Every hotel of a certain class the world over has hall porters or concierges who, although they may never have travelled, react identically to the vagaries of their profession. Every sergeant in every army, every constable in every police force, every Customs officer in every Customs house, has a similar way of being disagreeable. Only their affabilities are different, and often surprising. Every maitre d' has the same kind of vocational smile, and preserves the same precautionary distance.

We are, in other words, surrounded by an ever denser forest of stereotypes, uniform ways of doing things, and ever more desperate attempts on behalf of those who cultivate our imaginations for a living, to break out. A football match between the national teams of China and Kuwait would have titillated our expectations up to a few years ago. Today, it is scarcely different

43

from an encounter between Queen's Park Rangers and Manchester United. The players have learned very quickly to turn somersaults and leap over barriers when they score goals, and to form human totem-poles of delight which fall perilously to the ground. They have also learned to writhe in mortal agony while their aggressor is awarded a yellow card, then to hobble a few heroic yards, to receive a pass and streak towards the opposing goal as though nothing had happened. The crowd also has learned to break into atonal litanies in order to sting their team into action. And the referees all look as though they are remarkably well preserved for their age.

BEFORE THE START OF THE 1ST 4 x 100 METRES
RELAY RACE AT THE OLYMPIC GAMES

There is only one clear difference. Since both China and Kuwait are strictly national teams, there are no players totally black or totally white as there are in the English teams. Meanwhile, over the horizon, there is Boris Yeltsin tackling the vast reorientation of the Confederation of Independent States without batting an eyelid. It may be that Russia at this time of year is too cold for eyelid batting, but certainly a contributory factor to his nonchalance is the time wasted by his predecessors in assessing the immensity of the problem and therefore not knowing where to begin. Yeltsin seems to think it is better to do something, however rash, rather than to do nothing, however prudent. He is, therefore, probably right in treating the huge question of reorganization as run-of-the-mill.

Russia, after centuries of isolation, is resolved to acquire some of the cliches which entwine us like weeds in even our most private lives. She needs the comfort of passing through the phase we are in. We remember the ecstasy of British sports commentators when, at long last, the British 100-metre relay team defeated their American counterparts. The fact that all eight sprinters were black only heightened the patriotism of the commentators. When the Olympic team of the Confederation of Independent States boasts a handful of African athletes, as well as a sprinkling of Orientals, we will know that Russia has at last reached maturity in the increasingly unsurprising modern world. And to think there are still those who bleat about the dangers of federalism!

31 January, 1992

Party Time is Here Again

With ever more of the planet won over to the principles and practice of democracy, we witness continuously the struggles for ascendancy in very different systems, all dedicated to the freedom of the individual. Israel has just announced a date for a general election in early summer in order to try and shake itself free from a Knesset in a permanent state of deadlock, which consequently gives far too much importance to those representing shades of opinion in tiny backwaters of the mainstream.

In its broad lines, the struggle for public approval is between believers in obduracy on the one hand, who have made a bogeyman out of poor, homeless Mr Arafat, and those with sufficient self-confidence to have faith in flexibility and who therefore permit themselves to listen unflinchingly to the hugely impressive logic of Dr Ashrawi.

Add to this already heady mixture the minority in the backwaters, those who behave as though they are nodding acquaintances of God, and you have a scenario as eternal as the landscape and as exhilarating as aridity. The results of an election can hardly change much in this young and ancient state, at times cursed with excessive brilliance and benefits all round if only it were not so inhibited by the prevailing obtuseness.

The forthcoming elections in Tasmania, and in the federal region of Canberra, are even more acute examples of mega-multi-parties at work in small areas, with a glut of independents to confuse the issue in an electoral system of some complication even further. This democratic concern with faithfully reflecting shades of opinion is what frightens the British, in particular, and leads them to champion an obsolete system which believes in stability above all.

Opinion, they feel, can be safely relegated to two parties. Two is the minimum required for there to be freedom of choice, and to prove it, a third party artfully slipped under the wire before it could be stopped, and is now a permanent fly in the divided ointment, winning more in by-elections than it wins in elections, thereby confusing the issue.

There is no subtlety whatsoever about the British System; representation being the result of a winner-takes-all form, rather than anything as accurate or troublesome as the proportional. It seems as though the bigger the electorate, the less do the governments have the capacity to be as democratic as they pretend. On the huge canvas of the United States, there is none of the shading inherent in the choices of Tasmania, Canberra, or even Israel, none of the discreet *trompe l'oeil* of Britain; it is all glaring acrylic, as refined as Campbell's Soup seen by Andy Warhol.

The elections for a new, or old, president are beginning to gain momentum. For the world's most influential democracy, it is astonishing how much time is taken in preparing for and recovering from elections. The so-called 'Sweetheart Period' after an election, that period in which the incumbent is not blamed for his errors of judgment, is scarcely over before the jockeying and guile for the next test of strength begins. The polls ensure continuity by watching the standing of a president much as the weatherman watches his barometer, and the wretched man rises and falls on his roller coaster as exhilaratingly or depressingly as the Dow Average.

But there have been other developments. Mr Bush has announced that he will do anything it takes to win, a statement which might fill voters in some other countries with either trepidation or a gloomy sense of *déjà-vu*, but which in the United States represents nothing more than the trumpeting of a boxer before the title fight. There is, however, one new element to all this which might legitimately increase our anxiety about the future of the democratic process, if it is allowed to spread to other countries. Blackmail has declined recently, not because of any surprising advance in national morality, but simply because of a new system both safer, and, apparently, law-abiding. There is no need for the ugly business of kidnapping, and then all the

47

hideously risky rituals of messages left in obscure places, phone calls with disguised voices, and the eventual exchange of captive and the vast sum of money, if parties who will find themselves concerned wait until persons in the public eye present themselves as candidates for high office, be it as a presidential hopeful or a seat on the supreme court.

At that point ladies are discovered who suddenly remember sexual relations with the gentleman concerned, which were unbearably sordid and degrading. Today there is no need for insinuation or threat of blackmail. A convenient tabloid pays a sum for the story at least commensurate with that a blackmailer would have demanded, with only the condition that the money be earned by a properly pathetic and melodramatic comportment during the ensuing investigation. Whether the allegations are true or false, they are calculated to destroy the career of the victim. True or false, the accuser has been paid. True or false, serious papers can no longer refrain from quoting the offending tabloid once the allegations have seeped into the public domain and occasioned an enquiry.

Finally, that Gary Hart should have fallen foul of this procedure, whereas Judge Thomas survived it, and Mr Clinton is muddled but unbowed, does not alter the fact that no law seems to have been broken in this form of safe blackmail except perhaps that of slander, but fair comment is always given the benefit of the doubt in a country so proud of its freedom.

The sense of spurious piety awakened by all this is quite appalling. Once again, the truth matters not at all. A man's ability to govern well has rarely been affected unduly by his private life. Skeletons have appeared in the cupboards of many heroes past; John F. Kennedy, Roosevelt, Eisenhower. Anyone worth his salt has at least one of them. All that changes with promotion is the size of the cupboard, and of its keyhole.

6 February, 1992

A Man's World Down Under

Eighteen months ago, we sacrificed our European summer to tour Australia, going from one winter to another, albeit a mild one. Now we have had our revenge, abandoning the European winter for the antipodal summer. There are snow-storms and high seas, but only on the television news.

Outside it is all voluptuous sunlight with a sparkle in the air, a dappled pavement as the fierce light leaks through the magnificent trees, and people, loosely and functionally dressed go about their business, their faces screwed up against the insistent clemency of the elements, and the attentions of individual flies, who select their clients, and accompany them with the sudden devotion of stray dogs attaching themselves hopefully to prospective masters.

There can be few countries less addicted to tension than Australia. It has its problems, and some of them are grave ones. The Japanese car maker, Nissan, has just backed out of production here, liberating 1,800 workers into the ranks of the unemployed. There is nothing new about this. Nissan has merely made its exit along a well-trodden path, used previously by British Leyland, Volkswagen and Chrysler. The only unusual element is to see a leading Japanese corporation suffering a local reverse. Iacocca's revenge. The great economic uncertainty is a universal one, but because of Australia's distance from everywhere, the worry takes on a local colour. However, it is never discernible in people's attitudes, which remain unswervingly jovial, affectionately truculent, and brimming over with unsentimental goodwill.

It is perhaps typical that a great deal of newsprint is lavished on the desire of the Bishop of Canberra and Goulburn to ordain eleven women as priests, an initiative which was only stopped by a court injunction. This led to a religious retreat, and many photographs of eleven gloomy ladies meditating in the presence of Bishop Dowling.

Now the battle between the modern bishops and the traditionalists, who are opposed to this idea, has reached such proportions that it occasions a joyous confession by Mr Ivor Davies of Footscray, a reader of the *Melbourne Age*, who writes, 'I am glad to be an atheist. Fight on, religious fanatics, fight on'.

This illuminates no tendency apart from the Australian addiction to sport, at which they are extremely knowledgeable as spectators and superb active participants. It is typical that an individual with no special inclination towards the conventional aspects of piety should discern the favourable elements of a sport in the prattle of prelates.

Even without going to the lengths of embracing atheism, it is difficult at times for the laymen to comprehend the arguments in this cloistered conflict. I am grateful to Father John Potter, Melbourne chairman of a group opposing the ordination of women.

He declares that if Christ had wanted women as priests he would have chosen women as apostles. But then who admitted women as saints, which appear to me higher in the celestial hierarchy than mere clergywomen? And what about nuns, how did they slip through the net of masculine exclusivity? And is it not close to perversity to admit women to the highest echelons of the spirit, but to exclude them from the humdrum existence of the parish, a kind of *honoris causa* only for those whose devotional superiority is irrefutable?

And finally, is it not all a question of degree? Is not the mentality which denies women the possibility of a vocational call not the same which in ruder times prescribed the dunking and burning of witches, those unfortunates whose very unmale instincts made them receptive to the occult and invisible world, a world foreign to the tiresomely prosaic logic of the more insensitive gender?

It took a long time for women to get the vote, and there was no mystic reason for that eventual surrender. Some of the clergy think women are only out for another dose of their legitimate rights, and that rights have nothing to do with the world of the spirit.

Perhaps not, but it is certainly diminishing the horizons of the spirit to claim that this exclusive zone dealing with the agency and marketing of God's word is for men only, and that any vision invading the heart and soul of a woman must lead straight to martyrdom and sainthood, the agony of poetry as opposed to the routine of prose. Nobody is so bigoted that they still think there is no place in the church for women in some capacity. Could a man echo the thundering fragility of a Mother Theresa? Or convince in a voice as tiny but resolute as the unflickering flame of the tiniest of candles?

While this whispered battle rages for the solitary enjoyment of a single atheist in the gallery, an even more archaic accusation attempts to command our attention. Michael Thornton, described in the Australian press as a leading royal historian, blames the Queen personally for the monarchy's slump in popularity. She has failed most conspicuously, according to Mr Thornton, in her inability to lead her son towards a satisfying role as Prince of Wales, who is in danger of becoming a national bore. Mr Thornton sounds awfully like one of the intransigent clergy, suggesting between the lines that the Queen would have the Royal Family in much better control if only she were king.

Mr Thornton is welcome to his opinions, as I am to mine. The Prince of Wales' main drawback is that he is talented, which is perhaps the cruellest blow of fate for someone in his position, and the Royal Family do a hell of a job under the most trying circumstances, with men like Mr Thornton as arbiters of majesty, and tabloids short of subject matter as they are of circulation.

And meanwhile, 1.23 billion people are without clean drinking water, and 2.25 billion without sanitary facilities. A hundred million children don't know what a school is, and nearly one billion adults in the world are illiterate. Amen.

13 February, 1992

Villagers and Villains

Sydney Opera House has become a landmark, like the Eiffel Tower or the Rome Colosseum. Far more people know it by sight than have ever been in it, that collection of conquistadors' helmets close to the water's edge in the magnificent harbour, a monument to the depth and scope of Australian culture.

Two days ago, it performed a work which has become a classic of its genre although hardly associated in more tradition-bound shrines with opera at its grandest, *Fiddler on the Roof.* And to add to the anomalies, the lead part of Tevye the milkman in this dramatization of Sholon Aleichem's tale of Jewish village life in pogrom-ridden Imperial Russia was played by an actor, not, strictly speaking, a singer. The show received what are commonly known as mixed reviews from critics, their main beefs being levelled at the mediocre quality of the voices, the ensemble singing, and the slavish reproduction of Jerome Robbins's superb choreography. In other words, technicalities.

I must go on record as saying that, in spite of its alleged inadequacies, it was by a long chalk the finest version of the show I have seen. Let me go further, and declare that those very inadequacies made it so — not a polished, glittering feast for the superficial senses, but a deep and simple tale with a very pure emotional impact.

Max Gillies, a marvellous artist, made a very good Tevye, whose relationship with God approximated to that of a boxer to his corner in a countless series of rounds. Banished was all suggestion of the bittersweet, the schmaltzy, the ingratiating, the fatalistic. This elevated the consistently high level of general performance out of mere folklore into a deeper and essentially human experience. And it made the spectator realize the universality of the story.

The Russian villagers are not villains, there is even a hero among them. They are merely compelled to go through the motions of ruthlessness by the dictates of a grotesque autocracy, (and there are still people around who believe the revolution was unnecessary?). Is medicine necessary to combat an illness? It may have been the wrong medicine because of its after-effects, but was it worse than no medicine at all?

At all events, the Jews leave this troubled land with a quiet resolution to wander elsewhere. Only the busybodying matchmaker chooses Jerusalem, the others making for Warsaw and New York, where uncles are scattered like chaff. The relationship between hawks and doves has not altered with time, nor have the injustices in land described as occupied. Terror and deportation are symptoms of insecurity, then as now. This production should be required viewing for Mr Sharon and certain colleagues, not merely as a source of uplift. One of the best lines in the show comes near the end, as the family walk towards the sea with all their belongings on a couple of carts. Two children, with the insensitivity of their age, giggle and play, impervious to the solemn, even heroic atmosphere. The voice of Golde, the milkman's wife, cuts the morning air. 'Don't misbehave children. We're not in America yet.'

It seems only the other day that President Bush appealed for a kinder, gentler America. As a call, it always seemed tremendously civilized and a trifle unrealistic, simply because a recession is not really the ideal climate for whimsicality. In any case, he could hardly foresee the Gulf War, which appeared out of nowhere as a diversion from the economic anxieties. America was, then as now, eager to show what sheer military know-how could do for a country's reputation, now that the Soviet Union had slipped so thoughtlessly out of sight in order to try on a low profile for size.

After a slow start, the war was blindingly short, sharp and expensive. It was also inconclusive, which has made it long, dull and ruinous. And before it even started, General Dugan of the US Air Force was unceremoniously sacked for sharing his war aims with journalists. There was then a suggestion of a shadowy presence in all this, called 'Operation Decapitation'. Israeli sources had apparently suggested that the best way to hurt

Saddam Hussein was to target his mistress, his family, his personal bodyguard. Why all these and not the man himself? Well, obviously the United States cannot condone terrorism at a time when terrorism itself stands condemned, and nor can assassination, as such, be part of policy.

The result of these fine points is that whereas murder of an individual is out, murder of his entire entourage in the hope that he is in its midst is very much in. We remember this was attempted against Gaddafi, resulting in the death of a child, whereas Gaddafi escaped. The dismissal of General Dugan seemed only right at the time, even if no one bothered to refute his indiscretions. The trouble with them was that no doubt they were true.

The actual fighting came and went in a flash, ending in what I dared to call at the time, 'the usual collusion between good and evil in the worst of all worlds'. America went wild with celebration for a victory that was only half a victory. It was all based on the assumption that any normal country, faced with such a crushing defeat on the field of battle, would fire its leader and change the government. Evidently, Iraq was not a normal country, and Saddam, once he had been graciously let off the hook, is not one to get back on it again voluntarily.

So now what? After a series of miscalculations in which it was not too difficult to be wise before the event, Mr Bush has virtually taken out a contract on Saddam. Once again, we have the astonishing spectacle of a government taking an initiative which would cause immediate arrest if perpetrated by an individual. It is suggested that Bush wants Saddam to enter history before the elections. In a typically cryptic comment, a CIA official said that their new assignment was to fill Saddam's pants with sand. I have no idea what this means, but it sounds distinctly unattractive. Bush is not available for comment. He is too busy in his tracksuit again, seeming to overtake an Olympic athlete into the final straight for the press. Is this why it's called running for office? Okay kids. Misbehave. You're in America at last.

20 February, 1992

Turning the Tide in Hong Kong Harbour

Hong Kong harbour at six in the morning has all the misty quality of a Chinese watercolour, grey with subtle rosy tints, the turning in bed of a not-yet fully-awakened sun, attempting to snatch another few moments before rising. Closer scrutiny reveals the endless lines of traffic like pearls on an infinite rope, liquid still, but here and there stuck in a jam. There is no knowing when the hive of activity was set in motion. It is quite possible that it has continued from nightfall without interruption, that it is, in fact, Hong Kong's *perpetuum mobile*, rising to a crescendo during the day, never flagging completely at night.

This is an extraordinary anomaly by any standards. A city state of the greatest possible sophistication, probably more capable of governing itself than any other place on earth, which is still technically a colony while Pacific islands depending on bird droppings for their economy have achieved at least a nominal independence.

This absurdity, in part no doubt due to the nature of the ancient lease agreement with Imperial China, has led Britain to all manner of posturing on Hong Kong's behalf, without for a moment being able to conceal the intrinsic unreality of the situation. It is as though Hong Kong, now a fully grown adult of superior intelligence, were still relegated at times to wearing baby clothes.

Of course, all that will change in 1997 when the lease agreement expires. If it were not for that, the present peculiar status quo would be censured by every society living in the twentieth century.

And yet, ironically, the governing fear in the colony is to what extent things will change on that fateful day. Many have already left in the direction of Vancouver and San Francisco, among other cities with large Chinese communities, and there are huge corporations which, without abandoning Hong Kong altogether, have transferred their corporate headquarters to places such as Singapore. There are clearly people and corporations who believe an axe may fall, instead of a discreet blending process being allowed to take place. But at least, come what may, it will be an affair between Chinese and Chinese — not quite an internal matter, but at least one concerning a nation of brilliant pragmatists as well as political theorists continually adapting themselves to changing circumstances.

There will be no further cause for Britain to visit the headmaster of the new school in order to reassure herself that the pupil due in 1997 will not be victimized for evident scholastic superiority verging on genius. And there will be fewer embarrassments, such as selecting those worthy of British passports, or deciding which Vietnamese boat person is a genuine refugee and which is merely ambitious to become a millionaire in a more flexible society than his own. And there will be no more carrying those who fail to pass the arbitrary test, kicking and screaming on to aircraft for repatriation at a discreet hour of darkness in a city which never seems to sleep and which therefore recognizes no discreet hour of darkness. And finally there will be no more ill-concealed tensions between an outgoing governor of great lucidity and ability, knowing both the Chinese mind and language, and a government in London determined to deliver its charge to its new school personally, with a final admonition to both parties, and a reminder for the uncertain future, that nanny knew best.

Once the destiny of the colony is returned to China it is hard to imagine that the Peoples' Republic would be guilty of some precipitate action to devalue such a rare acquisition as Hong Kong. As it is, Hong Kong is influencing the mother country far more than being influenced by her. Already the free industrial zones adjacent to Hong Kong are benefiting from a welcome influx of foreign capital, whereas the very latest in the hotelier's art is manifest in many places on the mainland. Tourism is becoming an important industry as China has opened up discreetly and in her own time without needing any implorations for perestroika or glasnost.

On the contrary, she occasionally applies the brakes in order to remind the world who is boss, and we have ugly moments such as the sagas of Tiananmen Square. There are still vestiges of ancient callousness in the cold-blooded suppression of female lives in obedience to the one-child family regulation.

Such facts sicken our sensibilities, but it is predictable that, with all the miraculous means at our disposal in this information revolution, the more different parts of the planet begin to know about other parts, then the more nations will become aware of those norms of human behaviour which are generally accepted elsewhere.

It is certainly true that it is the immense size of China's population which leads to a relative cheapening of life, just as large European countries such as Britain, France and Germany, while often motivated by the highest social ambitions, have nowhere near the collective generosity of underpopulated nations such as Sweden or Norway. Size of population, area and climate play a primordial part in forming national character, and even in deciding religious adherence. Hong Kong is as indispensable to the Orient as Switzerland has been to Europe, and for many of the same reasons. There have to be such financial clearing-houses, seats of wealth and theatres of negotiation. Neutral soil is essential in such places.

All the same, some aspects of this extraordinary city may surprise the mainlanders when the border no longer exists. A highly cultivated and erudite gentleman sympathized with some of his Thai acquaintances the other night since they labour under a 600 per cent tax on luxury cars. Thank heaven, he added, the tax on a Rolls-Royce in Hong Kong is only 100 per cent. His smiling silence after this remark made it seem such a bargain that he was seriously thinking of having two.

5 March, 1992

A Punishment to Fit the Crime

As my tour of the Far East comes to an end and as an antici-
pation of Europe rediscovered begins to build in my mind,
I think it fit to register a few surprising impressions of a part of
the world with a centre of gravity utterly different from ours.
Hong Kong is well known for its extraordinary energy. Looking
down from a balcony at the impressive crowds of people, each
one with a predetermined reason for being where they are, and
for moving in a prescribed pattern, one is reminded inevitably of
the activity on an ant-hill. It all seems absurdly unmotivated and
excessive from above, this hysterical to-ing and fro-ing, and yet
each tiny element in the vast mob seems to have its function, like
cogs in an expensive watch.

One would have thought that such a concentration of
population dedicated entirely to the furthering of commercial
interests, representing every aspect from banking to gambling,
would have been pretty indifferent to spiritual values. They are
all too busy for those. And yet there loiters, only just out of sight,
a discernible spiritual hunger and an appreciation of things of the
mind and heart.

Oddly enough, this is manifest in its most primitive form as a
deep-rooted superstition, as ingrained as the mumbling of a
witchdoctor in a jungle clearing. When the ultra-modern Bank
of China building took shape, it was perceived that its jagged
form contained a kind of razor-sharp prow launched in the direction of Government House and more particularly aimed at the
Governor's office. All manner of sinister symbolism was read into
this fact, more especially in the light of the handover to China

in 1997, to say nothing of the Bank of China being a mainland institution. Ruffled spirits were only assuaged when a row of trees was transplanted to block the emanations from the aggressor edifice.

During my performance in the very contemporary theatre, an electric light bulb exploded over my head on the first night. It happened as I was coming to the end of a longish anecdote, and I referred to it as a point killer, raising a moderate laugh. The next night on arrival at the stage door I noticed the backstage staff in a particularly exhilarated mood. Apparently the theatre had been exorcised earlier in the day by an authority on the unseen world. It was, they assured me, quite safe to play it now. And although exploding light bulbs are a relatively rare occurrence in the theatre, the next three days were without incident.

Perhaps because of the proximity of China itself, there seems a sharper division between the native people of Hong Kong and the western elements than exist in Malaysia, a country more thinly populated and subjected to the ethical influence of Islam, with a strong whiff of the British public school in the background. A cheerful notice before arrival welcomes the traveller to Malaysia, at the same time warning him that drug-dealing is punishable by death. I was asked to surrender my passport on arrival so that a temporary work permit could be issued. Since there seem to be no theatres in Kuala Lumpur I was compelled to do my one-night stand in a hotel ballroom. The passport was returned to me later with the following entry: 'For performance as comedian at Concorde Hotel. Not permitted to sit out or dance with audience.' Since mine is a one-man show and I find it as difficult as even the inhabitants of Hong Kong to be in two places at once, it is hard to conceive of my being capable of sitting out while appearing, to say nothing of dancing with the audience.

Nevertheless, where hanging is part of a cordial welcome form, it makes me shudder to think what the penalties for unauthorized sitting out could possibly be. Dr Mahathir, the Prime Minister, was good enough to visit me during the interval in what I was told was my dressing room, and we had an interesting conversation, but I suspect he did not realize how close he came to flouting his own laws by talking to me at all. It came perilously close to 'sitting out', although luckily there was only standing room in the space accorded to me. Since I was not given a little bell to proclaim my social ostracism, I presume it was all just on the right side of legality.

Singapore has an even stronger savour of public school about it, exuding a feeling of contained opulence controlled by a puritanical sense of piety in its never-ending educational process for its people and for visitors. Here the welcome is as warm as it is in Malaysia; garlands of flowers greeting the new arrival. But the official guide on page 209 contained a more qualified table of punishments than the bold Malaysian reference to death as a penalty.

Here in Singapore under the Misuse of Drugs Act, trafficking, manufacturing, importing or exporting more than 15g of heroin, 30g of morphine, 30g of cocaine, 500g of cannabis, 200g of cannabis resin or 1.2kg of opium is punishable by death. Smaller portions of these entail between twenty and thirty years in prison and fifteen strokes of the rattan cane. Unauthorized traffic in controlled drugs other than those specified above warrants a minimum sentence of two years in prison and two strokes, to a maximum of twenty years and (wait for it) fifteen strokes. It seems almost clement.

Jay-walking carries a commensurate penalty of a $50 fine, while littering is subject to a $1,000 fine. As for smoking in public buses, lifts, theatres, cinemas and government offices, you will find yourself a mere $500 out of pocket. Chewing gum has also been outlawed, although no penalty for this abuse has yet been tabled. It is safe to assume, however, that unauthorized chomping will be penalized by somewhere between death and one stroke of the cane, possibly concurrent.

None of what I write has anything whatever to do with the undoubted joys of the hinterland and the intrinsic qualities of the various peoples comprising this part of the world. It is merely about the greater common denominator; those who learn from each other by sitting in air-conditioned offices and thinking up regulations to increase conformity and steer the human spirit into farmyard corrals.

A Malaysian questionnaire sent to me before my arrival asked: 'What depresses you most?' My answer was 'Official documents'.

Wisdom before the event?

12 March, 1992

60

Going Weak at the Knees

Whatever else it is, a painful knee is a confounded nuisance. I fell down a spiral staircase nearly two years ago because the dear lady who looks after me had polished the granite steps on the simple pretext that they looked better that way. Since I believe that there is a positive element concealed in every misfortune I must confess I had never known before the date of my accident that it was possible to fall down a spiral staircase with the same speed that one might fall down a straight flight of stairs. Well, I proved that it is possible. I took the seemingly endless curve with the acceleration and stability of a racing car, coming to rest on the floor below in a matter of seconds.

The result of this has been a feeling of uncertainty in cold or damp weather further aggravated by a one-man show which entails standing for almost three hours on the stage. It was not that the knee gave me any palpable trouble but I somehow heard distant rolls of thunder from its direction suggesting that it would take me by surprise one day.

It happened in the smouldering heat of Bangkok. I was on holiday and therefore wide open to treachery from this quarter. A car hooted too close for comfort in a narrow thoroughfare full of smiling gentlemen trying to sell false Rolexes. I spun around and felt a sudden agonizing pain. The car passed by and went on hooting at nothing in particular, more a bad habit than anything else.

The Thai doctor, a venerable lady exuding enormous and irrefutable wisdom, gave me a bandage, which was soon abandoned since it cut all communication between my foot and my thigh, and a multitude of pills, each of which was intended to counter the dangerous side-effects of the others. The situation improved and I was able to spend three weeks in blissful repose on a beach which was nevertheless 71 steps away from our hotel room. I negotiated each of these in both directions with the greatest possible circumspection.

Once the holiday was over, I began to perform in Australia and gradually the pain returned. In Hong Kong I had difficulty moving the leg and an extremely pretty therapist was summoned. She practised infra-red treatment and a subtle bombardment with laser-beams while I lay there perfectly content imagining that I was a switchboard in a seaside boarding-house.

Nothing very positive came out of this, and in Kuala Lumpur a doctor arrived in my room. He had a name so Chinese it sounded like a reverberating gong and he was the first to reassure me that there was no water on the knee. He gave me a bandage manufactured in Mauritius in which the pressure on the knee was adjustable. More creams appeared and I was handed pills to be taken in an emergency. Since I cannot imagine an emergency which does not keep one degree in reserve before reaching the limit of most extreme, I never used them.

In Singapore we lunched with a world-famous surgeon, who happens to be a personal friend. Out of a desire to help, mingled perhaps with curiosity, he examined my leg discreetly in the lounge of a distinguished social club. My knee behaved fairly well under the haughty scrutiny of past presidents, and my friend frowned at the emergency pills, claiming that they were old hat and dangerous to the stomach. Pausing at the hospital, he gave me other pills for that extreme emergency, which I have not taken either.

Back in Switzerland I went straight to a doctor who is also an osteopath to try and get to the root of the problem once and for all. He placed me on a table the size of a bunk in the crew quarters of a pre-war Japanese cargo ship. 'What I do to you here will either work or it won't,' he told me with commendable objectivity and then began to knead my leg as though he were a baker. I flinched and tried to avoid a too-direct pressure, but on a table which I overhung on both sides this was not easy.

After a time he asked me to lie on my stomach, and since nature has not been generous to me in the realm of daintiness the manoeuvre almost ended with a fall twice as dangerous as the mere bagatelle with the spiral staircase. After this treatment my knee no longer felt like an old wound which I would have to get used to. To resume what all these highly competent and independent authorities told me, it was essential to accept and act upon two great and complementary truths which govern accidents of this type.

The first is that no medicine on earth is a substitute for complete rest and, if possible, total immobility. The second is that within the framework of immobility a way must be found to continue motion. Walking, exercise, swimming are a vital part of the healing process and they must be judiciously added to the supine requirements dictated by logic.

In the final analysis, in this highly technical age the arbiter remains the instinct of the patient. Gone forever is the Olympian self-assurance of fifty years ago. In those far-off days the family doctor was an oracle whose sagacity extended into all the byways of medicine and whose verdict was accepted without question. There was rarely the need for a second opinion or specialist advice, especially with something as simple as a knee. You were to take to your bed and rest the damaged shock-absorber and he would be back on Wednesday morning. Now if you happened to die on Tuesday that was just too bad. It was his appointment book which was important, not an appointment with destiny.

Today, knowledge has expanded to the point of making both patients and doctors nervous. The more we know, the more there is left to know. The serene bedside manner is replaced by a vast compendium of doubts shared between patients and the doctors themselves. Diagnosis is drowned in a welter of alternative possibilities. The pundit no longer says: 'Take two after meals until further notice.' Today he is reduced to saying, as he produces a little phial. 'We'll try you on these. I'll give you six to go on with. Now listen carefully. If you start haemorrhaging during the night, stop the treatment at once and call me whatever the hour!'

Uncertainty has kept pace with technological brilliance which means perhaps that civilization is approaching maturity. While writing this I have been immobile. My knee feels quite normal. But what will happen when I move?

26 March, 1992

Where Charity Begins and Ends

The world of charity has grown even out of all proportion to the growth of population or of technology. Legion are the good works which seem to buttonhole the citizen with claims that this or that malady or affliction deserves precedence over all the others. Often this claim is emphasized by advertisements in newspapers showing, for instance, pathetic geriatric cases which seem to beg for a fragment of our comprehension, or pot-bellied babies in the laps of tragic, emaciated mothers, their anguished eyes staring through a mass of flies. These photographs have their effects on our sensibilities until such sights become common-place, and the advertisers seek some other way of claiming our attention.

After the initial shock, horror has a way of numbing the senses to the extent that the sudden apparition of a happy child in an advertisement is liable to have the same effect as that of the dying child before familiarity took its toll.

There are, of course, many more good causes than there are private resources to sustain them. I only have to examine my own mail to discover that quite 10 per cent of the letters I receive tug at heart-strings, or invoke a sense of historical continuity, or yet appeal to presumed predilections in my priorities.

All of the causes are worthy. Some are naturally worthier than others, though which are which I wouldn't know. I wish I could satisfy all those who grab my lapel through the post, but unfortunately that is beyond the capability of a mere individual. But would all this enormous effort be levelled at the individual at all if it were not for the failure of the collectivity, the negligence of governments which reserve resources for more important priorities than mere misfortune?

Occasionally, out of the murk of dire events like the rioting in Los Angeles, comes an image of such staggering clarity that it illuminates its subject. Here is a revolt so abrupt, so violent, that the government was forced to take a position and spend money. What it did was to send in 4,000 troops as a reminder of where the ultimate whiphand lay, and to reassure those who had already suffered that there would be an end to such unfairness. Here was something worse than an Act of God which unites those in distress. Here was an act of man which starts and finishes in disunity. There are those who see the basis of the conflict as racial; others see it a logical consequence of the numerous inequities in a society which its winners call free. Certainly, freedom to starve, freedom to be destitute, freedom to die on the sidewalk are included in the fringe benefits of a civilization addicted to growth and profit.

Nobody in their right mind would begrudge America its enormous natural wealth, and its apparently endless capacity for turning its potential to advantage. But the extent of abject poverty in a land so rich must be the object of shame and self-examination to those not entirely hardened by the belief that greed is good for you.

On the scale of charity the Americans are an object lesson for all. They are more generous than the rest of us, but then even in bad times they can afford to be more generous. That is, until events take over and compel the government to take a hand. I spoke before of an image which crystallizes the events as sure as the pot-bellied baby symbolizes the famine in the Sahel, but with perhaps even greater compulsion. A Swiss journalist, treading wearily among the fires and destruction in Los Angeles, came across a small boy crying bitterly. Under such circumstances it is normal to fear the worst. Had the small boy lost his parents, or worse, seen them killed? Full of trepidation, the Swiss journalist asked the lad what was wrong. Still sobbing, the little fellow blurted out, 'Every time I take a TV set out of a shop, some grown-up comes along and pinches it'.

That says it all. Call the riots racial if it suits you, or just a surge of the underprivileged. There are certainly such elements in the original impulse, but they soon became the kind of glee-ful hysteria we have known in our football crowds and in the young cretins who steal cars in order to smash them. And how will the little boy grow up in the shadow of such memories? He will certainly carry with him the deep sense of resentment of an honest looter who was deprived of his earnings by those larger and rougher than himself. His sense of justice may be left intact, but applied to other values. And it is to be feared that later on, when he commits his series of murders — because that, like looting, has become fashionable — he will go to the gas-chamber after many years of bureaucratic fine print, bitterly resentful to the end of a society so basically corrupt that it favours the big and strong over the small and helpless.

Where does individual charity end, and where is the collectivity forced to take over? Has the potentially distorted mind of this small boy no claim to our attention, alongside the hospices for the dying and those reduced to vegetable life by the ravages of cruel diseases — or the million-and-one worthy causes which drop through the letter box round the clock? There are remarkable individuals already, and in surprising numbers, who do more than their share in the alleviation of suffering and the creation of a sense of fraternity between the smitten and those conscious of their luck in being of sound limb. And there are organizations which have risen out of the historical inability of governments to assume responsibility.

The Red Cross was the inspiration of an individual sickened by the sight of battle in Napoleon's time. Les Medecins sans Frontieres, Greenpeace, Amnesty International, all started with seemingly slightly disreputable maverick images, only to gain not only respectability, but also authority with the passage of time. By now, it is impossible to conceive of contemporary society without such necessities thrown up by need. What then of all the others, and that small survivor of the riots, empty-handed and embittered? The sight of the dead, either wet with firemen's hoses or leaking gasoline in the red night of LA, or lying in positions of supplication in the bright sunlight of Bosnia, cut off in the middle of a shouted order or a comradely greeting, are deeply sad and depressing. But the mind is quite as fragile as the body, and its death is quite invisible.

What next? Some pious platitudes from Mr Bush about the way Barbara and he feel about it? A determination not to make political capital by Mr Clinton, in what sounds quite like political capital?

How can they seriously understand the cause or assess what is needed so close to an election? And how can they assess after an election in the warmth of a sweetheart period? And unfortunately there are other things to think about later, among them the next election.

In the last resort it's up to the individual as usual. Stoop to pick up the mail on the welcome mat. This envelope looks as grim as the others. Courage!

14 May, 1992

The Good and the Great

There are moments in life when the roving eye and vagrant ear are confined to barracks for an enforced reassessment of their capabilities, and the mind is purged of all inessentials in a moment of truth which sharpens the focus to a point of almost unbearable clarity. I've had several such moments in my life. The birth of each child registers the fact that nothing will ever be quite the same again. There is a new element to consider, a new character will be forming in the shelter of the nest in order eventually to join in the struggle for survival, armed I hope, and hoped, with a few parental virtues, and unhindered by too many parental vices.

On quite another level, the outbreak of war was another such moment. That first wailing siren, over a London still wedded to the fretful activities of peacetime, was so unreal that people who had been advised to go to cellars, or at least shelter under tables, went out onto balconies to await the latest developments. It was a false alarm, I remember, like so many others. The real alarms were often upon us before we knew it, although the Greek chorus of the sirens became our constant companion in the long dark night.

There was a pamphlet warning people what to do in the event of an attack by mustard gas. We were advised to move the casualties as quickly as possible from the affected area. How rank amateurs were supposed to know the confines of an affected area was never stated, nor was it indicated what protection was needed to enter such an area, once it kept still long enough to be recognized for what it was. All the pamphlet would let on was that victims of this obnoxious weapon should be treated to a cup of hot sweet tea.

The reading of this pamphlet was another moment of clair-voyance, in which it was suddenly obvious to me that the world was changing gear from a stately speed to a precipitated and hideous one, in which human values and elementary decencies would be manhandled, hot sweet tea would be replaced by acid, conversation by screamed sophistry and the music of the spheres by dive bombers.

The focus was unbearably sharp at that moment. The most recent incidents of such a palpable stillness in the landscape of the mind occurred last week, when I was accorded the great honour of being elevated to the rank of Chancellor at the University of Durham. I knew the previous Chancellor, Dame Margot Fonteyn, by virtue of having painted many of her ballet shoes for the Sleeping Beauty in 1938. I literally held her foot-steps in my hand before daring to put my clumsy feet where the ground was only marked by traces of her pointes. That it was a great responsibility I knew in advance, but I could not guess at the pervasive atmosphere of the place itself. Now that it is over, I can admit to having abandoned my formal speech after the dress rehearsal in the Cathedral, where I was exposed to the magically warm atmosphere of a place which, by virtue of its gothic splendour, could so easily have remained cold.

The singing of the choir, the fanfares of sundry brass instru-ments, the clear diapason of the organ, all contributed to bring life to the ancient stones, creating an envelope for the ritual at once majestic and miraculously accessible or, as I put it, at once human and super-human. The whole short, almost terse, affair, struck a balance which once again made me conscious of a sharpened focus. An appreciation of the past lends credibility and confidence to a vision of the future.

While in Hong Kong recently, I had already been entertained to lunch by the Durham University Alumni Association, numbering seventy-nine members. What they had to say about the place was both moving and unexpected. It was without exception affectionate. This foretaste was confirmed in the University itself.

I'm not suggesting for a moment that such characteristics are not shared by other seats of learning. After all, I only have experience of two, Durham and Dundee, where I was rector some twenty years ago, but have since revisited. In both these universities I was struck by the maturity and individuality of the students. I must say more so today than in the heady 1960s when graffiti were the eloquence of the moment.

One student last week asked me why I had accorded an Honorary Degree to Alexander Yakovlev, described by the excellent orator public of the University as the architect of Glasnost, still advisor to Mr. Yeltsin, and father figure of the emerging Russian democracy.

As the orator said he was the son of a man in extremely humble circumstances and his mother could neither read nor write, I replied somewhat robustly that this is exactly the kind of man whom a university should honour, and to whom it should extend its appreciation as an exemplary member of the human race. The student then gently chided me, declaring that he was in favour of my gesture, only wanting to know why I shared his opinion. Ah, conditoned reflexes. How often one pre-supposes that which is not there!

Those selected for *honoris causa* degrees were to my mind a perfect mixture for this joyous occasion. Glenda Jackson, so quietly resolute on the eve of her second career in the playhouse of Parliament; Leon Davico, an old and tireless colleague from UNICEF, UNESCO and the High Commission for Refugees, just back from a mission of mercy in Sarajevo; and of course Terry Waite, that miracle of human endurance and unflinching dignity, owner of a most infectious and disconcerting guffaw which could scarcely leave any captor indifferent.

All four new doctors have lived their lives according to their principles and sense of values, and they grace the university with their spirit. Now it is over, the focus relapses into soft. Other facts of life crowd in. And yet, I can never forget a day in which it all seemed clear. Most important, I can relive it at random in the mind.

21 May, 1992

The Right to Bear Arms

As everybody knows, America has just lived through an experience which would have been traumatic in any smaller or more tightly organized country, but things have a habit of drifting into the background of the mind over here.

They even have a phrase for problems which are urgent, but not as urgent as the business of living. They say that they are put on the back burner, a culinary image as graphic as it is at times, depressing.

Ben Hecht, the famous journalist, said words to the effect that today's newspaper, however cogent or graphic it may be, is only fit for wrapping fish tomorrow.

People forget if given half a chance, and headlines are ephemeral. In a country consistently dedicated to the latest technical novelties, among them cable television, with a choice of sixty channels in the Chicago area, no head of steam is ever allowed to build up sufficiently to disturb the equilibrium of the half-ways affluent citizen.

Newspapers are so copious that it is virtually impossible for a working person to read more than a fraction of them. This glut of images and information, as well as of rather bland editorializing, leads to a mentality both unquestioning and glib. Of course, there are those who are deeply disturbed by the drift of events towards what they see as an unavoidable and dramatic crisis in the life of cities, but they fill the airwaves with the jeremiads and hideous warnings of what is bound to happen if nothing is done, to the extent that there are always more entertaining channels to switch on to, and these voices are generally unheeded among the

71

welter of jolly talk shows and lucrative parlour games.

There is, by European standards, too much of everything here for anything to take more than a momentary grip on the mind. Of course, the riots in Los Angeles frightened and disturbed Americans even more than they did us; but to the question of what is to be done to resolve the problems of inequality, the answer is slowly crystallizing into a cosy nothing.

The president is seen looking at the debris with a grave face, and that may convince those who still equate a grave face with concern, but the creation of sub-committees and even task forces is eventually merely lip-service towards the anxieties of the public, and the photographs of yesterday's conflagration wrap today's fish.

In truth, many believe that such outbursts of fury, engendered by the now notorious amateur video of a black gentleman being belaboured by the night sticks of the police, and the subsequent acquittal of the police by a largely white jury, are merely a superficial sickness of society's skin rather than a graver internal disease; eczema rather than cancer. And it can certainly be interpreted as an isolated eruption in a nation addicted to the pursuit of happiness, armed to the teeth, and caught too often in the crossfire of gang warfare.

The equivocal gun laws certainly add to the ambiguities of the sacrosanct Constitution, so tirelessly invoked to define the rights of the individual. The Founding Fathers decreed that every man should have the right to carry arms in the interest of self-defence, but they were thinking in terms of flintlock pistols which took quite a time to reload after the first shattering and inaccurate discharge. Those wise men cannot, in fairness, have envisaged machine guns and bazookas as means of self-defence, and it is the purest hypocrisy to attribute today's jungle law to their foresight.

In fact, eye witnesses to the Los Angeles riots were unanimous in their horror at the quantity of firearms which appeared in private hands. The gangs themselves are a far cry from the racketeers of the prohibition era, the Mafiosi with vested interests in gambling and prostitution. These no doubt still exist, but they have acquired a counterfeit patina of reticence and decency.

The gangs today are composed of under-privileged young people of both sexes, imposing on themselves a strange discipline and loyalties which they never enjoyed in broken and transitory homes. In the saddest possible way, these young people are trying to fight their way back to a kind of normality, by these horrible and arbitrary means. And in this area, where understanding and compassion are so desperately needed, they meet only the strong-arm methods of an often discredited police.

It surprised some that the Korean community were perhaps the most evident target for the outrage of the African-American and Hispanic rioters. The Koreans are relative newcomers to the celebrated melting pot of the United States. The descendants of African slaves have evolved slowly from their original degradation to their present status, furnishing many large cities with mayors, and the nation with eminent public figures and successful businessmen. The prejudices, now largely unspoken, still exist as regards the mass, even if the elite is no longer subjected to the kind of unpleasantness prevalent even a quarter of a century ago.

As a nation, the United States has succeeded more than the wildest expectations of optimists had led them to expect, and even if race relations are by no means perfect, a great deal that is good and positive has undeniably been accomplished. Hispanics have been part of the scene ever since the early growing pains, with the acquisition of Texas by the United States and the punitive expeditions into Mexico.

Compared to these indigenous minorities, the Koreans are late arrivals, without complexes. With the advantage of novelty, they understood the system prevailing in their new homeland, accepted it, and exploited aspects of it which had been neglected by native Americans.

All-night fruiterers and greengrocers sprang up all over the place, supplying a demand, and bringing solvency and later wealth to these new capitalists. And finally, they understood the system so well, that they acquired a plentiful supply of weapons on the open market to protect their way of life.

Fiction and reality mingle ceaselessly on sixty channels of television. Pray heaven this immense country does not too often confuse truth and half-truth, justice and plea bargain, patriotism and chauvinism, for all our sakes.

28 May, 1992

The Price of Forgiveness

It is impossible to place a value on human life. This seems to vary according to region, to tradition, and to awareness of changing values.

I must say, it is a disagreeable surprise to be working temporarily in a land which has, in the main, retained the death sentence for the punishment of so-called capital crimes. I am no longer used to the discreet horror of this adjunct to a quality of life which deems itself civilized.

Let me place my cards unashamedly on the table. I do not believe that any country which still preserves such primitive solutions to an age-old problem deserves the description of civilized. In that sense, the United States, a gigantic land with a communal abstract dream, is still, in the main, uncivilized and backward. Out of fifty states, only eleven have renounced the finality of mortal justice.

If I refer to primitive solutions in the plural, it is because there are many alternative ways of being executed in the USA, according to the state in which the crime was committed. The majority today prefer lethal injections, although the electric chair still has its partisans; while the firing squad is theoretically utilized in Idaho, hanging finds favour in Montana, Washington State, and Utah, and three states, among them California, allow themselves to be inspired by the Nazi nightmare, and plump for the gas-chamber.

Ever since public executions were abolished, presumably because they excited the morbid side of human nature, these odious ceremonies of extinction have been kicked under the

74

carpet to be performed in sinister isolation, with only a handful of officials present. Now they are creeping back into the open again, as a consequence of the information age into which we have entered.

Today, we do not see the actual moment of death. That may well come with the irresistible march of entertainment to envelope all branches of public life, including politics and religion — and once all public life is show business, why not public death?

But for the moment, we are only regaled with that which leads up to the fatal second. Quite recently, a young man called Roger Coleman was electrocuted in the state of Virginia. Up to the last moment, influential news media pleaded his case with the greatest energy. Time magazine placed him on the cover. 'This man might be innocent,' it read, 'this man is due to die.' The editorial, which covered four pages, was extremely effective in casting doubt on the case for the lack of any save circumstantial evidence, and pointed to many anomalies, or possible anomalies, along the way.

If there is so much as a shred of doubt, why the hurry with an irreversible decision after ten years of waiting while the various avenues of appeal were being exhausted?

The answer is perhaps furnished by another item in the same magazine, reporting that the Supreme Court is restricting access to appeals for Death Row inmates. The justices have ruled that federal courts are no longer obligated to grant a hearing on appeals, even if the inmate can prove that his lawyer failed to present important facts. This seems to signal a kind of exasperation with the vast and complicated legal system, in which over 2,500 prisoners are lining up like taxis on a taxi rank, waiting for their turn to die.

Another consideration in this terrible untidiness has to be the enormous expense of keeping such people alive, and of listening to their endless appeals in a system which attempts to reconcile unflinching humanity with inflexible firmness. It fails on both counts. Truth cannot be subjected to time limits, nor can doubt be forcibly deprived of its benefit. And meanwhile, the appeal has become one to the public itself, rather than merely to legal pundits.

Mr Coleman appeared regularly on television for the week before his execution. We quickly began to recognize him and to understand his unique and ghastly predicament. He protested his innocence almost negligently, and spoke of the reasons he could not possibly have been the culprit. Without knowing all the details of the trial it would have been gullible to be convinced by his story, but at least what he said, and especially the way he said it, held water and compelled the attention.

More so than the rejection of the appeal by Governor Wilder of Virginia, standing on a lawn, blinded by the sun, and talking in a dull monotone about his desire to be humane under such circumstances.

With my European squeamishness, I admit to having found it difficult to concentrate on the stage the night of Mr Coleman's execution. I kept consulting my watch. I anticipated a reprieve. It did not come. I felt I had known him, and would recognize him in a crowd. And then I remembered the extremely long telegram I had sent Sir David Maxwell-Fyfe, the Home Secretary in the British government at the time of the Bentley murder. I set out the reasons why it was quite wrong to hang a young man called Bentley because he had allegedly, by a shout, encouraged an under-age youth to shoot a policeman. I neither had any influence on the outcome of the verdict, nor did I engender as much as a terse acknowledgment from Sir David's office for the ardour of my plea. Now, many years later, Bentley has been posthumously exonerated from blame. It was an error of judgment. I derive absolutely no satisfaction from this irony of fate, feeling only sorrow that at the time Sir David was too important a legal figure to pay attention for a moment to an unimportant by-stander. And it fails to reassure me about the case of Mr Coleman.

The *Chicago Tribune* came to the surprising conclusion that the media had less clout than had been imagined, for failing to influence the course of justice. This may be true in the vast open spaces of America, in which the destiny of Mr Coleman is quickly forgotten in a welter of sports scores, commercial messages, and more recent murders. In countries of European dimension, heads of steam are allowed to build to the point that many previous legal decisions have been recently reversed, and the very structure of justice is under the severest scrutiny.

There may well be those who ask why I lavish all this concern on single cases when there are events like the riots in Los Angeles or Bangkok in which many were killed, among them innocents.

Well, we have no direct control over riots, but a death sentence is the responsibility of all in a society.

We can still, however, learn wisdom from cultures other than our own, faced with similar problems. The Bangkok riots ended when the king amnestied all concerned as the price of re-established peace. A Thai professor explained the success of the king's action. 'Buddhists are quick to forgive.' The weeping widow, over the coffin of her assassinated husband in that horrendous Mafia assassination in Palermo, sobbed, 'I'd forgive them, if only they'd change'. There is the whole weight of the Christian ethic. What price an eye for an eye and a death for a death?

4 June, 1992

Stability and Stupidity

From the relative neutrality of Canadian soil, I can look back with amazement at the prowess of Mr Ross Perot, the self-made billionaire, who leads President Bush and Governor Clinton in the polls by an amount so considerable it can scarcely be the error it seems to have been in Britain. He is accused by his detractors of never making a policy statement, but he quite simply answers that he has no wish to lie like every other candidate. He also says he has no thought of abusing his opponents. He may not have, but when Dan Rather of CBS asked him if he would be willing to emulate Mr Bush in saying 'read my lips' instead of answering a question, Ross Perot roundly declared that nobody would catch him saying something quite as stupid as that.

As you can see, he is a most unusual candidate in that he is not a candidate at all for the moment, merely a spoilsport, or the early warning of a deliverance according to the observer's inclinations. All his smoke signals proclaim his candidacy; and yet he refuses to fight on a battle ground not of his own choosing; nor will he be rushed by those who believe that the time to crush him is now.

Mark you, it is always possible that his bubble will burst, or at least dwindle to a soapsud once he formally declares that he is in the race for office. Maybe his impressive showing is due to the threat of running, and that the elaborate framework of common sense will crumble once he has lowered himself sufficiently to compete with others in a world of sordid reality.

Whatever happens, it is the grotesquely complicated structure of checks and balances, the permanent hymn to stability which is to blame for the cumbersome constitutional procedures of American elections, at times reduced to total immobility. And, of course, this very immobility, induced by a Democrat majority in the House and a Republican President, enables someone as down-to-earth and nimble as Mr Ross Perot to have a field day in the petrified forest of once mobile men. All he really has to do is to point out the absurdities of such a situation to inspire immediate support for that no-nonsense homespun wisdom so beloved of those who dream the American way.

In that sense, Mr Ross Perot, with his short, spare figure, is reminiscent of Harry Truman, the kind of regular guy who drives his own venerable Oldsmobile, believes in personal contact even with the road, and who backs his own hunches to the hilt, because the alternatives don't make no sense. Sometimes I think he is a prosaic wizard, invented by Shakespeare in a visionary moment, whose name is P. Rospero. Time will tell.

Meanwhile, as the Americans realize that whatever happens the system must be properly ventilated in order to function, British eyes are once again glued to the keyhole. Whether the contents of the new book about the state of the principal royal marriage is fact or mere prattle matters little. What matters much and is profoundly depressing is the public interest in such degrading gossip. There is speculation in some papers as to whether the institution of royalty can withstand such shocks. To judge by the vociferous and glutinous reaction to this story, the monarchy is an eternal and solitary skittle, always available to be knocked down at times when there are no real stories worthy of record.

Certainly this book, to judge by the published extracts, is exactly the kind of initiative the Royal Family are at such pains to prevent by compelling butlers and nannies in their service to sign agreements that they will never indulge in the selling of stories for profit once they have left the royal service.

To doubt the utility of a monarch as an anachronism in modern times is a matter of opinion. But to use it as a permanent and reliable target for mud slinging is both unpleasant and undemocratic, reflecting on the character of a nation. Undemocratic because the right to personal privacy on any level of society is a more precious one than the public's right to information — all too often the public's right to mis-information.

And meanwhile, Denmark surprises the world, and no doubt

itself, by voting, by a narrow margin, against acceptance of the Maastricht Treaty. As a convinced European I suppose I should feel appalled, but in fact I feel a sort of relief that it has happened now. Why? Because a small nation, Denmark, shared the fear of many more populous ones that its very identity would be threatened by the centrifugal force of a United Europe. Now, in managing to throw a spanner into the works, she has proved exactly the contrary. The emerging Europe is immensely respectful of democratic rules, and Denmark's surprising decision is accepted as one which is the prerogative of any nation whatever the size of its population or its economic strength.

What happens next is anyone's guess, but one thing is sure, and that is that Denmark and many other participating countries have been relieved of a complex by the immediate acceptance of the fact that a small country's vote is of equal importance to the vote of a large one. This can only bode well for the future.

A less rosy note is struck in Slovakia, eager as are so many other small people for an independence which will not prove to be one at all. United forcibly by a Treaty of Versailles signed in different times, by statesmen with less meticulous aims than are necessary today, the manufactured countries of Central and Eastern Europe have been held together by a growing but superficial force of habit, and by superstructures which effectively congeal their status quo. Even the Soviet Union, which disintegrated with astonishing despatch, reformed itself with equal urgency into a confederation of independent states, with happier results for the time being than those in Yugoslavia. Independence cannot exist economically in times in which even great powers are interdependent; it can only be enjoyed within the amicable structures of a law-abiding interdependence. To yearn for independence today is an old-fashioned illusion and, where it is based solely on racial considerations, as in Serbia, it becomes both foolish and, when pressed to its logical conclusion, criminal.

The sinister racial rubbish of the Nazis is there as an odious example for all those in search of purity and elusive genetic tidiness.

The conclusion of all this? Perhaps that, although intelligence is only rarely rewarded in this world, stupidity is no valid substitute for it.

18 June, 1992

Of Vandals and Values

When moving from place to place these days, one is never very far away from evidence of man's brutality. The savagery in Los Angeles is marked by scars of recent origin, with all the ugliness which that entails.

As always, there are details which remain in the mind when the original impression is quickly registered and conveniently relegated to memory. The detail which struck me most forcibly was an announcement on the charred wall of a shattered supermarket; now as lovely as a broken tooth in a vagrant's mouth, spelling out the words 'Tropical Fish' in fancy lettering. It was impossible not to imagine the reflection of the flames in the glass of their bowls, the permanent panic expressed in their target-like eyes now given an understandable justification. The first bubbles of heat must have appeared in the water of their world, as round as Colombus's but far less promising, until it was dashed to the ground where the gorgeous translucent blues, dazzling reds and vibrant yellows were reduced to drab cinders, their astonished eyes being the last elements to go. I can never, from now on, think of the rioting without this image of loathsome insensitivity. Even if excuses can be conjured up to justify frustrations with the immobility of the establishment, it is difficult to understand why tropical fish, who have little to offer but their beauty should become the victims of gratuitous hooliganism.

But then it is all very well to judge these things from the point of view of a concerned normality. It is difficult for those with minds trained to be active in the hard school of experience to understand the sheer boredom brought about by the insulation of ignorance. The young men in search of a cause as easily under-standable as insane loyalty to a football club's colours on a muf-fler, and eternal chants from the cheaper seats, are the same as those who cried for Nero's thumbs down sign in the Colosseum so that they could suddenly live out their fantasies in the sight and sound of death.

Naturally, opportunities were restricted in those far off days. There were few parking problems because people came to the games on foot, even if the first mule minders must have been already active outside the entrance gates. Today, when even the poor find it possible to travel on occasion, the virus of inactivity spreads far more readily than before. Surely one of the delights of travel is to be subjected to other climates, other eating habits, other ways of life.

To bother to go all the way to Sweden in order to export your own dim vision of reality, and end up brawling in a place as inspiring as a beer tent, in order to inflame the mind to acts of heroism against riot police, shop windows or other champions with allegiance to other colours and other discordant chants is an abuse of the opportunities offered.

But come to think of it, the only opportunity the poor had to travel in the past was as members of the armed forces. They were mobilized by officers in much the same way as they mobilized themselves into units today. Then they enjoyed the privilege of foreign travel but only in order to desecrate the countryside, degrade the environment, kill as many foreigners as possible or be killed. In that sense the activities of the football supporters are an atavistic return to ancient values. Since armies are gradually falling out of fashion and military intervention is on the wane, joining up no longer gives the opportunities for travel that it once did. That role is now played by football-supporters clubs. And if today the arrival of these dangerous youths into a town inspires the same fear in a local population as did boorish regi-ments of centuries past, pillaging and ransacking as an officially approved reward for hardships endured, there is a very good rea-son for it. They are virtually the same men. Then, volunteering for the armed forces was a way to break the deadlock of slum life. Today the situation is almost worse for the human spirit. The perils of penury have been transformed into the terrible monotony and endless humiliation of life on the dole. The threat of starvation is no longer there, but the assault upon basic human dignity is worse than ever, a sense of slavery to the grudging generosity of the community being among the soul-destroying elements of unemployment. And small wonder that there are misguided outbursts by those who seek to lend life a little excitement by smashing things. They give ample warning of their intention to be different by shaving their heads, wearing earrings or punching studs into their noses. Unfortunately, in being different they only succeed in resembling each other, and we are back again to the concept of the regiment, eager for conflict and the imposition of the extreme sacrifice of others. Politicians are incessantly talking of strong-armed methods, reinforcing the police and so forth. This is as facile as it is fruitless. There have been many government schemes in many parts of the world, usually gathered under the generic heading of job creation, which sounds awfully like the sergeant major designating an extra ten men to spud-bashing. Where the powers that be have singularly failed, however, is in the realm of the imagination. Little has been done to break the soul-destroying monotony of the kind of existence which cannot be gratified by the name of life. The human mind only functions if it is engaged, and it does not take too much to engage it or to stimulate it. Imagination may be elusive, but it costs nothing.

Young Mr Dan Quayle, the American Vice President understands this. He is among those who wishes to bring order into the prevailing chaos. He speaks of family values as though they were inventions of his own, even if his juvenile face and visible effort to be categoric by slow, deliberate enunciation are calculated to inspire pride in appearance and a smile of disbelief in practically everybody else. Never mind, he knows the value of education and of good education in particular. Visiting a school in the course of his re-election campaign, he entered a classroom while a class was in progress. A small boy stood at the blackboard. In answer to a question the boy spelled out the word p-o-t-a-t-o. Mr Quayle then demonstrated those qualities of leadership and attachment to cultural values to which he lays claim, by kindly giving that small boy the benefit of his experience. Taking the chalk he added an 'e' — p-o-t-a-t-o-e. Now we k-n-o-e.

25 June, 1992

e pluribus unum

Prague once again. Events have gone quicker than one's sense of normality allows. Such is the development of collaboration in Europe that a flight announced as Air France 2044 from Paris to Prague turns out to be Czechoslovakian Airlines with some quite different number. This cooperative effort exists equally with airlines presently well outside the European Community. The last leg of my homecoming on Sunday night will be an internal flight with Swiss Air from Zurich to Geneva. It is announced as Austrian Airlines Flight 213.

My reason for being in Prague in the first place? A meeting of the World Federalist Movement for a Just World Order Through A Strengthened United Nations. Quite a mouthful for quite a mindful. And what has it to do with me? For better or for worse I was elected President. And there is no better place to hold such a Congress than Prague, and no better moment to hold it in than now. Among the honorary vice presidents are such luminaries as the erstwhile independent US Presidential candidate John Anderson, the explorer Thor Heyerdahl, and the violinist and pedagogue Sir Yehudi Menuhin, and on a most distinguished list of past presidents there is Norman Cousins, a truly great American.

There have been considerable efforts in Britain of recent months to make federalism into a dirty word, much as the Americans have managed to translate one of the noblest words of the English language 'liberal' into an epithet for feckless *laissez faire* and indifference to national imperatives.

These are distortions as odious in their way as the rape of that wonderfully expressive word 'gay', which has transformed it into something far removed from the original intention, something defiant and on occasion even sad.

Well, such distortions are typical of the times we live in. Any great step forward sparks off its own reaction. At the very moment in which the most powerful nations in the world are discovering the illusory nature of independence and the virtue of that further step along the road to a general enjoyment of liberty called interdependence, small nations, several generations behind the leaders, are crying for that independence which is no longer viable economically, or practically.

In earlier times the tendency was to coalesce, to form powerful empires like the Roman, the Persian, the British and the French. Even the latecomers like Germany and Italy found their Bismark and Garibaldi to preach the gospel of unity, culminating in the ultimate decadence of imperial power, with the disasters of Hitler and Mussolini, whose fall provoked the final curtain on the ideal of Empire the world over.

Now, with the collapse of centralized and unreal economies in the East, and a crisis in the capitalist world which refuses to go away, the nations are despite themselves edging towards interdependence and by definition towards the federal solution.

It is a fundamental error to consider federalists in any way political. They may have colossal rows among themselves of a political nature, but that in itself is proof of the apolitical nature of a movement more linked by an ideal, however distant, than divided by transitory considerations of a political nature. Our concern is at no time the acceptance of this or that political credo in which individuals may well believe, but rather the creation of a vehicle for the enjoyment of peace under law, and the survival and encouragement of national idiosyncrasies and various beliefs within the safety of an independent structure agreed by all for their mutual benefit.

A pious hope? Not if common sense and magnanimity still carry any weight in the affairs of men. At this moment the Slovaks are voting their independence from the Czechs. Now, admittedly the Treaty of Versailles, still imbued with the spirit of the last century, sought to salvage what it could from the Austro-Hungarian empire by forcibly creating states without much contribution from those directly concerned. The Czechs, Slovaks, Moravians and Ruthenians were lumped together to form

Czechoslovakia, whereas Slovenia, Croatia, Serbia, Montenegro, Bosnia-Herzegovina and Macedonia were stitched together to make Yugoslavia. It seems as though neither of these improvisations is destined for survival.

Hitler shrewdly played on the frustrated nationalisms within Czechoslovakia by making so-called Bohemia-Moravia a vassal state, rigorously and cruelly administered, whereas Slovakia was given the illusion of a relative independence under the leadership of a fascist priest, Father Tiso. It was a cunning exercise in one-upmanship, and even if the rot did not set in at that moment, it was at least kept alive. Now, under the leadership of Mr Meciar — like Mr Milosevic in Serbia, a lightly disguised apparatchik from the previous regime, and eager to preserve some of the privileges and disciplines of those regretted days — some Slovaks are apparently opting for a course which, under the banner of a nominal independence, will bring infinite hardship in its wake. Independence does not only mean a national anthem to sing or a flag to salute. It also means an ability to attract foreign investment and a valid economic base for survival in a world lacking in tenderness.

Already Estonia, Latvia and Lithuania, independent in name but in dire financial straits, are decreeing that a knowledge of their respective languages is a prerequisite for nationality. This is, of course, aimed at the 35 per cent Russian minorities long resident on their soil. But where will the fervour of independence end?

Will aircraft approaching Tallinn Airport be compelled to address the control tower in Estonian, or those about to land in Bratislava in Slovak? If this silliness continues we will have, as I once predicted, 400 proud flags fluttering outside the UN building in New York, hardly distinguishable from each other in the appalling congestion, at least half of the nations represented unable to pay their dues, or even a decent salary of a delegate. Should Czechoslovakia disintegrate, the Czechs will come out of it far better than the Slovaks, having no difficulty in attracting foreign investment, and enjoying a reputation for industrial skill. It will be tragic if independence comes to be identified with empty stomachs. At least with interdependence, independence stands a chance of being enjoyed.

16 July, 1992

The Shape of Things to
Come?

Change comes with the erosion of established ideas, like the tireless gnawing at cliffs by the sea. Our concept of the future is often felicitous, because we cannot foresee the emergence of new textures, of new techniques and consequently, of new appearances.

To see futuristic films of years ago is a nostalgic rather than an enlightening experience. 'Things to Come', if I remember rightly, had the majority of the actors dressed in Perspex, and one can imagine few materials less adapted to the movements of the human body. There is never a hint of today's micro-technologies in all of Jules Verne's massive dreams, his submarine seeming to contain drawing rooms, libraries, and other necessities of decent Victorian existence.

In other words, reading the future in physical terms is not one of mankind's strong points. Nor can we foresee exactly the kind of retro-quirks which taste will undergo at any given time. At this moment, for instance, there seems to be a general architectural reversion to the style of the Crystal Palace, an influence of Fin-de-siécle greenhouses, simplified and sterilized to meet the esthetic demands of the day.

The road between London and Heathrow airport is rich in buildings marrying brick with mock-moorish domes in glass, whereas Munich's new airport is one enormous conservatory, painted like an undercoat, redolent of the hidden parts of thermal establishments before the Kaiser's war. If it is difficult to anticipate images of the future, or even images of the past, resuscitated as a background for the present, it is even more of a challenge to try to understand what was normal for our ancestors or what will be normal for our descendants.

The novels of the last century or the plays of the Restoration or Jacobean periods are full of rich characters with whom we can still identify today. In a sense, by virtue of his rigour and the extraordinary discipline of his writing, Molière is as contemporary in his appeal as are the best of today's writers, and if Shakespeare is approached without that reverence he never solicits, his genius is eminently accessible.

And yet we may imagine a judge, a contemporary of Dickens, who is a model husband in the mould of the period, as respectful of his wife's needs as he is insistent of his own, a beloved father to some intimidated and silent children, seen but not heard, and a stern but just employer to his domestics. He never forgets an anniversary, and his voice always rises above the chorus when it comes to hymns and carols. And even if he is musically a little uncertain at times, he knows every word of the texts, a fact of which he is inordinately proud. He knows far more about the classics than is usual today, and he can even invent a tolerable pun in Latin, or else enjoy a conundrum in ancient Greek. And how and where does this paragon of ancient virtues spend his working days?

In court, occasionally having to condemn children to death for stealing wallets, the black cap perched almost negligently on his wig. There is no time and no need to warn them never to do such a wicked thing again. If you were to pale in his presence and splutter in horror and disbelief 'a child?', he would only reply with a wintry smile and a fatalistic shrug, 'Well, after all, sir, a wallet was stolen, and to be more lenient would be to create a dangerous precedent. Indeed, one shudders to think of the consequences.'

Well, standards do change, but in light of this change may we ask ourselves what the reactions of people in a hundred years time will be, when they contemplate us with the raised eyebrows we reserve for the normalities of yesterday. It may well be discovered that murder and sexual depravity are curable illnesses if detected in time, and that privatized hospitals become more fashionable than privatized prisons as places of rehabilitation. It may even be that in a civilization undergoing an increasing presence of homosexual and feminist militants, heterosexuals will become a guilt-ridden minority. These speculations may well be as erroneous as were the Perspex skirts in the film half a century ago, but it is at least certain that the values of the immediate future will be as different from those pertaining today as these are to the values of the immediate past.

There is on record the voice of a French Cabinet minister, speaking not long after the First World War, and speculating in vibrant tones on the patriotic fervour in the heart of a French mother upon discovering that the unknown soldier is none other than her son.

Such a fantasy would hardly wash today. One is reminded of the brilliant reflection of another Frenchman, not a politician this time, but a comic, the late lamented Fernand Reynaud, who once said that wars are fought by people who do not know each other on behalf of those who do know each other but don't fight. This kind of trenchant irony has by now permeated all our ideas about patriotism practised at the expense of others. In an epoch in which cold steel and the single bullet have given way to the possibility of utter obliteration and the poisoned earth an aftermath, a new set of values has emerged even in the infinitely hazardous area of modern warfare.

The Gulf War unveiled a whole arsenal of intelligent weapons, bombs which sniffed at targets like tracker-dogs, only doing damage when it was justified, and other wonderful fruits of lethal ingenuity. Once the war was over, or rather invested with a long and uneasy intermission, it was discovered that the weapons were a little less intelligent than had been imagined, that the destruction was neither as thorough nor as selective as we had been led to believe, and that many lavish claims had been exaggerated. Never mind, at least the effort towards a humane sort of conflict was manifest, however absurd such a contradiction might seem in the light of friendly fire and other results of human fallibility. This official squeamishness has developed as a consequence of the perfection of nuclear weapons, and the fear of their passing into unauthorized hands. When war was merely total they preferred their bombs stupid. The stupider the better.

Thousands of these rained down on Dresden some fifty years ago, destroying a city of great beauty, containing practically no factories and no military installations, but thousands of refugees from more obvious targets, including children.

A statue to Air Chief Marshal 'Bomber' Harris (Dresden was his baby) was unveiled not long ago. Yes, standards change with the passage of time, but in a world inherently unstable times tend to overlap. And then, nobody wants to be remembered by a pile of rubble.

23 July, 1992

News from the Balkans

Among the wide range of mail which tumbles through the letter box every morning, there is something for every taste. There are demands for autographed photographs, almost exclusively from Germany, where this activity has reached industrial proportions, albeit as a cottage industry. Then there are brochures extolling the cultural activities of smart hotels, such as exhibitions of appalling kitsch in the foyer, and, of course, a few personal letters and many requests for financial aid from eminently worthy causes.

This endless flow of lava onto the welcome mat almost succeeds in spoiling breakfast, that most welcome and most succulent meal of the day. Every now and then, an arrival helps to ease the monotony. Easy to recognize by virtue of its drab cover, the colour and consistency of frozen porridge, a copy of a weekly newspaper lands on the floor with the welter of other mail. This happens every two weeks, which you may think odd for a weekly. The easy explanation is that it comes from what is, was, and may be Yugoslavia, where time limits are not easily understood.

Ferocious battles seem to break out at the very second of a ceasefire, negotiated for the umpteenth time, which fact has even succeeded in creating friction between the resilient Lord Carrington and the possessive Secretary-General of the United Nations. If such may be accounted among the successes of double-talking Balkan diplomacy, why not have a newspaper billed as 'The International Weekly', with, in smaller letters beneath the title, 'Belgrade, July 18–31, 1992'? It is all part of the same logic. In fact, this weekly is not without interest, for it

91

is published by the highly reputable daily paper *Politika*, which has evidently retained the possibility of independent opinion even in these hard times. First of all, it is a relief to find a paper totally unobsessed with those stray bits of tinsel which succeed in blinding us to more important issues. The present edition is perhaps a little early for a Yugoslav view on Mr Mellor's problems, but one knows in advance that the next issue will be too late for these. And in any case, there is no journalese here so immature as to describe the alleged distraction from Mr Mellor's straight and narrow as an out-of-work actress, suggesting with the poisoned coyness of a Victorian spinster that had she been employed she would have had no time for the fruits of idleness.

All this puts me in mind of my own family tree, collated by a group of old Russian ladies as a duty. It is a work of absurd thoroughness, only failing deliberately with two obscure relatives, one of whom, a male, married what is described as 'an actress', and another, a female, who shacked up with 'a Bolshevik', both left anonymous for reasons of propriety. If the team of old dears were still alive and active, I can't help wondering what kind of veil would be drawn over my own activities.

But to revert to more important matters, the sudden apparition of Mr Milan Panic on the Serbian scene dominates this issue, his smiling photograph, with both fists raised, gracing the front page in colour. The legend reads, 'Born to be first', and it comes as no surprise to learn that this distinguished Californian biochemist was also, in his time, a cycling champion, for his gesture on the photograph is exactly that made by those crossing the line first in the Tour de France. He has been rightly compared to Mr Ross Perot, exuberant in his optimism that sound business sense will sweep the pride and prejudice of mildewed Balkan bosses from its path. His arrival on the scene has had the same effect as Elliott Ness might have had, had he entered Chicago with a brass band and floats full of showgirls in order to ensnare Al Capone in a spider's web of technicalities. In questions from reporters as to how he intended to proceed, the answers would have been alternatively 'Don't bother me with details,' and 'God help Capone if he gets in my way'. Impressive as determination; a little less impressive as reality. An article by Ile Kovacevic, entitled 'On The Road To Hope', puts the situation in focus. 'Yugoslavia has lived through its last days for years, defying the logic of both East and West. The reduced Yugoslavia now has a Prime Minister who advocates peace, and claims that you will succeed only if you privatize the economy and introduce Western evaluation criteria. An almost fantastic picture has thus been portrayed: doves of peace flying among the hawks who have devastated the Yugoslav economy and are now perched on cold smokestacks, protecting empty plants from Western intruders.' It is clear from both this and a full-page advertisement taken out by the Association of Managers, that speech is still free in this strangest of dictatorships, with its superannuated Communist president and its Serb-again prime ministry. The advertisement demands the end of the war and economic blockade. It demands normal life. It also insists that political change is necessary. The page offering useful information is indicative of a grim adhesion to the ideal of normality. There is a list of the new authorized border crossings between the Federal Republic of Yugoslavia and Macedonia, Bosnia Herzegovina and the UN protected area. There is an advertisement for the zoo, open from 8am till 7pm, and apparently unthreatened as is its British counterpart by insolvency and closure, or, to quote Milan Panic, Western evaluation criteria. There is a crossword puzzle, and advertisements for at least three McDonald's. There are innumerable concerts and theatrical performances, including a rather ominous announcement 'At midnight Marijana Arsenijevic will perform Chaupin (sic) waltzes'. The weather forecast, no doubt accurate, is unstable and warm. The back page of the paper is perhaps the most astonishing of all, constituting as it does an interview with the Crown Prince of Yugoslavia, which is both lucid and down-to-earth. He regrets never having been accorded an audience with the elusive Milosevic, although granting that close contacts with luminaries such as Mulroney, Hurd and Mitterrand is some compensation for this ice-cold shoulder at home. Full marks for an excellent interview with an out of work monarch from this unemployed actor. British tabloids and Russian dowagers, please copy.

30 July, 1992

Games Without Frontiers

We are in the middle of the short, voluptuous, dangerous, silly season, the time when the weather is traditionally at its best, when great wars are started by the militaristic spoilsports who deprive the public of its well earned holiday.

One is tempted to believe that humanity has crawled too far along the rocky road to maturity to indulge in such imbecilities again, or rather imbecilities on such a scale. Today, we only have a little war, in which armistices are a daily occurrence, followed by brisk artillery bombardment, and skirmishes the world over. As a substitute for their nefarious stimulus we have the Olympic Games, a fitting monument to the pig-headedness of the past as well as an antidote to them.

Barcelona, as everyone knows, is the second city of Spain, as well as being the capital of Catalonia, a province speaking its own ancient language and always teetering on the brink of autonomy not to say independence.

The relationship between the two peoples and the two cultures was expressed with exemplary tact during an opening ceremony redolent of local and national pride, but never of chauvinism. After a complicated mythological ballet, as mysterious as the mists of time themselves, there was the traditional parade of the participants, a geography lesson in itself, as well as a charming demonstration of that sense of occasion inherent in every human being of goodwill. It was pleasant to see the parental pride on the faces of the Spanish Royal couple as their son strutted jauntily by bearing the banner of the national team.

It was also a refreshing surprise to see Fidel Castro looking relaxed and even happy after the daily struggle for survival of his beleaguered regime. This is not an expression of political prejudice but merely one of humanity, and humanity, not politics, is what the Olympic Games are all about.

The real Olympic spirit is felt among the competitors, those who know the difficulties inherent in the ferocious disciplines to which they are exposed, and have no time for the denigration of the weaker, even if they are unstinting in their praises for the stronger. The level of grace and elegance in the statements of the participants is consistently high; the only notes of ugliness emanating from the commentators and the media, fulfilling their chosen function as debunkers of idealism, and reminding us that the real world is very different.

I happened to watch the opening ceremony on French television and I wish I had not. Not that I allowed the commentary to interfere with my pleasure. At the same time it was impossible to ignore what the gentlemen were saying to each other. Mind you, the French pride themselves, not without reason, on their imagination and sense of style, but that really should not blind them to the qualities, even in diminished quantities, in others. After the superb abstractions of the inauguration of the Winter Games, and the gargantuan ceremonies celebrating the bicentenary of the revolution, they evidently feel themselves qualified to be the judges of what is good and bad in others. One of the French commentators called the Catalan opening ceremony '*Bon-enfant*' which is about as patronizing as you can get, suggesting that whereas the intentions were the best, the realization of excessive ambitions was woefully inadequate and unskilled.

At another moment, one of these authorities made a particularly outrageous reflection on the quality of the organization, only to be piously called to order by the other saying, in a voice filled with indulgence and caustic amusement, 'I think it's a little early in the day to cast aspersions on the Spanish capacity for organization'. The inference being, of course, that sooner or later this would be inevitable.

A leading French newspaper referred to the elements of folklore, and the astonishing performance of Spanish (mainly Catalan) singers in great arias from the operatic repertoire as Kitsch.

It is unusual for any nation to be able to muster, on a single platform, artistes such as Monserrat Caballe, Placido Domingo, Alfredo Kraus, Jose Carreras, Joan Pons and Teresa Berganza. One remembers that in Paris, to do justice to the Marseillaise, the great Jessie Norman was temporarily imported.

Lest it be thought that my strictures are exclusively aimed at the French, I must state that ill-luck has resulted in my doing most of my television watching on French channels, but that on the rare occasions on which I have caught a commentary in English, it has tended to gild an all too fragile, and indeed broken, lily. 'The British athlete is at the moment in eighth position', one hears, 'but he is in touch with the other.' There are, of course, eight competitors in the event in question. The athletes themselves often preserved a puzzled look in victory, especially in swimming events, as though they had emerged from a long stint in a chlorinated Hades, to be blinded by the sudden glare of mortal sunlight as their fingers touch a magic wall. Only the pundits are able to say that his or her performance is a disappointment after that remarkable showing in Hemel Hempstead in 1983 when he or she was eleven years old. The presence of ex-champions among the ranks of hardened sports commentators is an excellent development, adding a dash of personal experience to the factual authorities and patriotic bias of the commentators.

Human nature being what it is, it is far too early to eliminate the playing of national anthems from the ceremonies of the podium. The moved faces of some gold-medalists are eloquent testimony to their motivation and the consummation of their ambitions. After all, this is the civilized substitute for war, appealing to exactly the same instincts as those which lingered in the heart of the Neanderthal man, and which haunt us to this day. The difference being that here the damage is confined to broken legs, broken ankles, broken arms, hamstrings, ligaments and even broken spirits, but only in the rarest misfortunes to death.

In every sense the Olympics are a tremendous advance on war, and compared to the firebrand patriots of the past, the TV commentators are on reflection, merely amusing.

6 August, 1992

New Worlds and Old

On the face of it, it seems like a wonderful idea, and certainly one would do all one could for Liverpool, a great British seaport, which has had more than its fair share of carping, with the radical left seeming to outweigh the Beatles in those suspect scales of justice.

As an initiative, a fanfare for a new world is indeed a bold one. First of all, it is out-of-doors. With a background of a forest of masts belonging to the tall ships in the harbour, celebrating the climax of the grand regatta Columbus, the largest tall ship race ever held, a stage has been constructed, resembling yet another ship, albeit a grounded one. This is a safe precaution if one hopes to enable some of the great voices participating in this gala to stay in tune, unaffected by lurching or sudden swirls of the current.

Also, with a grounded ship, the relation with the audience and the artist remains constant, a vital aid to enjoyment. The organizer of the concert says that, quite apart from commemorating Columbus's discovery of America, it also salutes the emerging 'new world of the new Europe', but most importantly, it signals the new world which is opening up for Liverpool and Merseyside as a result of the opportunities of the single European market.

Ah, there we have it! Not content with the previous abrasiveness for those who see Trotsky loitering in the vicinity of every little incident, Liverpool now fearlessly demonstrates her farsightedness, and what the Americans are pleased to call her 'enlightened self-interest'. There is nothing wrong with this. It merely proves how far we have all travelled along the road to harmony, the radical left and the radical right notwithstanding.

97

Now that we are close enough to one another to be able to see eye to eye, we often do. The presence of the King and Queen of Spain at this celebration invites one to reflect how the course of history might have been changed had the sailors of the invincible Armada been invited ashore instead of being engaged in battle. One result might have been the inclusion of bowls as an Olympic discipline. The game on Plymouth Hoe would probably have been won by the home team, since they knew every tricky little inflection of the ground, and had had plenty of time to practise, while the ponderous floating cathedrals of the opposition were still busy finding out from what direction the pitiful little whimper of wind was coming.

In any case, in those far-off days, it took such a superhuman effort to find your enemy that once you were within reach, there was no alternative but to fight. Nowadays, you can find the opposetion in a matter of minutes, and since conflict on a modern scale is suicidal, both sides have no course left open but concord.

And there we have it, the King of Spain, fresh from the triumph of the Olympic Games in Barcelona, is now actually on British soil, joining in a celebration which, at the time of the discovery of the New World, would have been unthinkable. Why? Well both sides had their pride, divergent religious temperaments and their Italian favourite sons.

Cristoforo Colombo dutifully became Cristobal Colon, and beat his northern rivals to the punch. The British have never liked to be bustled out of a temperate appreciation of events — a glimpse at Lord Carrington or Douglas Hurd at work is enough to realize that nothing in this tradition has stirred for centuries — so that when news reached London that Columbus had planted the Spanish flag and a crucifix on a bit of *terra incognita*, it set off one of those sober panics which makes the British at times so dangerous and so unpredictable. The first acquisition in the preparation of a counter-blow was an Italian navigator of their own. Giovanni Caboto was found, and he quickly became John Cabot. A shrewd choice, it was thought, since he had three sons, and Britain might, with luck, acquire four explorers for the price of one. Letters Patent were duly drawn up by what must have been a solicitor in the service of Henry VII. These documents gave John Cabot, and his sons Lewis, Sebastian and Sanzius, 'full and free authority, leave, and power upon their own proper costs and charges' (it is here that we sense a whiff of the notary) 'to seek out, discover and find whatsoever isles, countries, regions or provinces of the heathen or infidel, which before this time have been unknown to all Christians'.

It is a strangely modern document for all its antiquity, never using one word where ten will do. It is further stipulated that any merchandise materializing from those unknown isles, countries, regions or provinces, could be imported free of duty through the Customs at Bristol, but although the whole great adventure was to be fully underwritten by the Cabots themselves, the King reserved for himself, at no risk, one fifth of the net gains from the transactions. For all the meticulous legality of the documents, none of the parties had the remotest idea what they were doing.

Cabot intended to discover the isle of Brazil on his way to Asia. This was deemed to lie far to the south of the islands upon which Columbus had planted his crucifixes. The solictors were wary and declined even to limit the potential discoveries to islands. Cabot set sail from England on May 2nd, 1497 and landed on Cape Breton island on June 24th, inadvertently discovering Canada, which he firmly believed was Asia. He planted the royal banner of England on the headland, and returned to Bristol on August 6th. The King was simply delighted by the news and rewarded John Cabot with ten pounds.

One would have liked to have heard the arguments in counsel leading to a decision about the exact sum to be paid. Possibly the King initially suggested fifteen pounds; wiser counsel prevailed, pointing out that Cabot was basically a foreigner, and therefore an adventurer by nature, and that he could easily let success go to his head, and be of no further value to his adopted country. 'What do you suggest?' asked the King. 'Five pounds?' suggested the Chancellor of the Exchequer, his lips hardly visible by virtue of their compression. The King commented acidly that such a sum would affect his reputation as a sponsor, rather than be detrimental to Cabot's vanity. 'I will be regarded abroad as one who tips rather than as one who pays for services rendered.' Eventually a happy compromise was reached, as it usually is. Ten pounds. I can hear the voice of a contemporary solicitor, his glasses aglint with combativity 'Mark you, ten pounds then was not at all the same sum as it is today'. Let me assure him, that as compensation for the discovery of Canada, there is not that much difference between the two sums.

And here we are today, in the midst of a never-ending recession, spending money as though the banks had just enjoyed a bumper harvest. First of all the Olympics, and the glorious informality of their last hours, and now the reckless generosity of a great city, dedicated to the best of all causes, that of humanity.

The dreadful obscenities in Bosnia, a temporary aberration, unites us in horror, simply because we have advanced so far from instinctive obedience to our primal instincts, towards common sense.

20 August, 1992

Idle Threats

Holidays clear the mind, and make one sensitive to the grace notes of life. Observed from the deck of a beloved sailing boat — built in 1929, of an age to be a brother — a small German boy afloat, about five years old, wearing water-wings and a cap, and screaming his lungs out. His scream was not prolonged but staccato, a cry of distress rather than of panic. Not far off in the water, the father, red-faced with embarrassment at all this noise, wagging a warning finger and rasping in German 'All right, one more scream, and Daddy doesn't swim with you anymore!'

The little boy could scarcely believe his good luck. Summoning up his remaining strength, he let out what Saddam Hussein would have described as the mother of all screams. The father added no words, just lifted his son bodily out of the sea, and dumped him on the deck. Last seen the child was burbling happily to himself, and eating a banana. One wonders, naturally, if the same errors of judgment are practised in more influential negotiations, for instance those opposing the militant Serbs to the rest.

Once again, in the stucco Mediterranean palace momentarily housing my wife, who does not wholly share my passion for boats, but prefers beaches, there is a short, overcrowded drive leading up to the rotating doors. On it, I encountered three gentlemen from the Gulf, arguing volubly among themselves, and consequently making very little progress. I was at the wheel of my car, revving-up politely, and was reduced eventually to giving a short stutter on the horn. Nothing doing. It was more hazardous than a snail's pace, because every now and then, to emphasise a point, one or other of them would step backwards. When at last I was able to stop and get out from behind the wheel, I was in time to hear the most authoritative of the three begin a verbal assault of unbelievable proportions on the liveried doorman. 'Why is my car not here when I want it? I said in front of the door. Instead, it has to be fetched and I am forced to wait.' There followed a catalogue of vituperation, comparing the door-man to the lowest forms of animal life, and threatening divine retribution for such gross negligence towards a superior being.

I was so incensed that I vented my anger on the man, shout-ing my repulsion at his attitude. This had as little effect as the klaxon. He simply ignored my outburst, and walked away, hesi-tated for a moment, and then returned to press a hundred-franc bill into the doorman's hand.

'I've known him for ten years,' confided the doorman after the client had walked away again, and while a minion ahead left at the double to fetch the car. 'He doesn't even live in the hotel, but in a flat nearby. He merely comes here to use the beach. He's the secretary of a potentate, who is politeness itself, usually because he's too sozzled to do anything more provocative than smile. But this fellow has made it a habit to treat me as an animal, but always over-tips me when he's had his pleasure. What am I sup-posed to do but give him satisfaction? I daren't complain, because his tips go a long way up the ladder; and anyway, I'd be out of pocket, wouldn't I?'

This disturbingly kinky ritual also opens one's eyes to behav-iour which is deemed to be normal in parts of the world where wealth and position make their own laws, and where contact with them by porters, however unpleasant, is considered a privilege worthy of a pittance.

After all, they weren't waiting for Godot, but only for a Rolls-Royce. The next morning, emerging from the hotel to await my car like any normal mortal, I was in time to see a gleaming black Corvette drive up, looking like an avenging instrument out of an American wish-fulfilment soap opera, abristle with hidden guns, and possessing a discreet capacity for flying over traffic when urgency demands it. The car was not parked, mark you, but left arbitrarily on the drive, thereby inviting traffic to accumulate behind it; and it was not Batman who struggled out of the door, but a hefty fellow wearing nothing but a baseball cap and tattered blue-jean shorts. He entered the hotel without a word to anyone. He was evidently very far up whatever hierarchy it is. The doorman rushed to the car in order to try and move it, since a line of hooting vehicles had developed very quickly, my own at the end of it, still in the main road. The doorman was immediately lost to view behind the black-tinted windows, but the convulsive movements of his charge suggested that he was more used to Citroens. Eventually he managed to force it, belching with unused power, onto a pavement, out of the way. Before he had time to attend to the other cars, the hefty fellow emerged from the hotel, talking quietly into a mobile phone. The doorman, proud of a job well done, held open the door of the car he had just struggled out of and made a sweeping gesture, inviting the hefty gentleman to take his place at the wheel.

The latter, still engaged on the telephone, walked past the black Corvette, sat down in a BMW convertible, and drove off noisily. With rock music at full volume on the radio, he had no need to hoot to make his presence felt. This client was above oral contact with the lowly to get his kicks. More exalted than a mere secretary, he derived his pleasure by being at once above contact, and seeming to own everything in sight. In fact, I wondered if the secretary's car had not been relegated to the car park simply because all the cars outside the hotel were there, awaiting the hefty fellow's whims.

And so, holidays draw attention to the exercise of power to which we are, in the main, unaccustomed. At the same time there is a change of emphasis in those news items which we know only too well. While they lasted, the exploits of Fergie around a local swimming pool caused very little attention, perhaps because the French, unlike the British, care little who is sucking whose toe at any given time; and to put this startling revelation down to the public right for information is the kind of prim hypocrisy which so endears Britain to her detractors.

If it were America, there would no doubt already be a movement piously entitled 'Paparazzi For A Clean Society'. They would have their work cut out with Woody Allen, who is already being treated as a democratic hopeful by the more unscrupulous Republicans. These suggest that a roving eye and wayward heart are palpable symbols of liberalism, and that an open mind can only lead to iniquity. As if that were not absurd enough, those logical French are reduced, by pressure from the mass of their usually ineffectual politicians, to treat the referendum on Maastricht as a pseudo-political election, whereas, of course, it is considerably more far-reaching and important than that.

Let us hope that as a final rallying cry, to place at least the fiscal interdependence of Europe beyond a doubt, President Mitterrand won't in his turn be reduced to the miscalculation of 'one more criticism and Daddy won't swim with you anymore!'

3 September, 1992

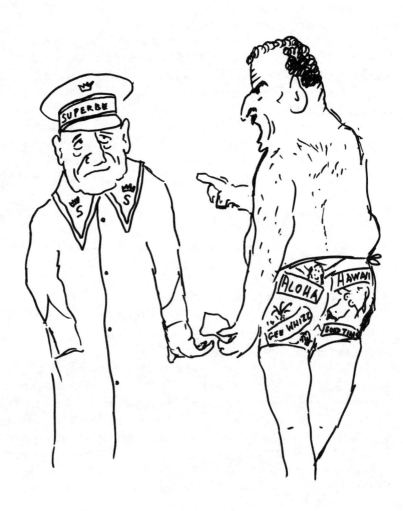

States of Mind

I was astonished, not to say shocked, to read an editorial opinion in *The European*, displayed boldly on the front page, advising the French to vote 'non' to Maastricht.

My surprise was certainly conditioned by the fact that I was in at the paper's birth, was present throughout its near terminal illness, and am still there to witness its healthy adolescence. It is not unnatural for one with so rich and so intimate an experience of a living entity to possess almost proprietary feelings towards it.

In this spirit, I read on to discover what on earth had driven the Editor to come down so harshly against a treaty to which both dreams and nightmares are so firmly attached, both euphoric and ominous. 'For all our sakes, *The European* hopes they will throw it out and insist that the politicians and bureaucrats go back to the drawing board', is what I read.

Not for my sake, I reflected, and went on with my lesson. 'A treaty which will shape the lives of every European for generations to come should not be implemented unless it has the whole-hearted consent of the people in every member state.'

The same could be said of every treaty ever signed between two or several states, but there is no historical precedent for such a ridiculously rash and Utopian initiative. Already, by asking for the whole-hearted consent of the people in every member state, you are guaranteeing that such a treaty, however much work there is on the drawing board, will never be signed at all.

Already, the politicians and bureaucrats have worked far into many nights, and have managed to produce as the fruit of their labours a document which few have the intelligence, and even fewer the patience, to read down to the fine prints. Everyone agrees that it is imperfect, and some even maintain that it can never be anything but imperfect by its very nature. In the light of these assessments, I would suggest in all humility that to expect even a revision of this document to acquire the whole-hearted consent of the people in every member state is an absurdity.

Most people in their senses wouldn't be caught dead reading a treaty as a pastime, and even if they were compelled to, it could hardly engender whole-hearted consent unless there were an ugly threat attached to it. 'The Danes have voted against the Treaty', we are told. There is no mention of the fact that the Irish have voted for it. The score is not love-one but one-all.

The editorial continues graciously, leaving the front page to important news like 'Dogs for Dinner Shocks Swiss', and relegating itself to the page traditionally reserved for the joys of bias and finger-wagging. We read that 'Instead of finding out what kind of Europe their people wanted and then trying to draft a treaty to meet these aspirations, the politicians and bureaucrats put together a private deal after months of secretive wheeling and dealing'. What, pray, is the machinery for finding out what kind of Europe their people wanted? A series of endless referenda driving whole populations up a pole, or perhaps a barrage of the fashionable and misleading polls of the other kind, ending up inevitably with the 'don't knows' outweighing the 'yeas' and 'nays' in the absence of provision for the 'don't cares'?

And why should negotiations suddenly be categorized as wheeling and dealing behind closed doors? If, indeed, this wheeling and dealing has culminated in a treaty which is, according to the editorial, 'so loosely worded that the British Government can sell it as a return of powers to member states, while the Germans present it as a step towards a United States of Europe', then this loose wording is deliberate, and was pragmatically the only possible compromise between the prejudices of its promulgators.

This can lead us to only one conclusion, which is that ratified or unratified, the treaty will be subject to endless negotiation and re-assessment until such a time as it makes way for a further advance in the integration of our Continent. Some might say that if this is true, it matters little whether the 'yeas' or the 'nays' prevail. On the contrary, it matters a great deal. The treaty is an emotional issue far more than a legal document prepared as a grazing ground for highly paid nit-pickers. Youth is very much in need of a cause, which its elders have never found an urgent necessity.

Europe, as a step to demonstrations of real fraternity and ecological awareness, all the idealism so readily described as woolly by those more concerned with the observation of life's petty decencies, is certainly a pressing argument for a massive 'oui'. A 'non' is but a surrender to all the guilt-edged insecurities of yesteryear, nostalgia for custom shed and barrack yard, attachment to increasingly worthless national currencies, and the illusion that a cold, unhygienic room is the man on the dole's castle. Eventually, 'non' and 'oui' are reflections of states of mind far more than approval or disapproval of details in a document. It is remarkable how many captains of industry are in favour of Maastricht, seeing in it the only logical way out of the present parlous economic situation.

Of course, a unified currency would certainly remove a lucrative playground from those speculators who assure their own prosperity in this century of the middle-man. What is worse still is the amount that is lost in the transfer from one currency to another by those whose work entails a collection of revenues from different countries. But these are details compared to the main drift of the argument. Towards the end of the editorial, we are warned 'Let no one say that a vote against Maastricht is a vote against Europe. The community will continue to grow with or without a Treaty'.

I beg to differ. A 'no' vote will be treated like a defeat for Europe, whether *The European* likes it or not, a 'yes' vote will be binding in its main thrust, but still be open to interpretation in the nature of languages, more so in the English version of the text than in the French.

If the Treaty of Versailles, or any treaty for that matter, had been submitted to the whole-hearted consent of the people in every member state, they would never have been signed at all. So much the better, did I hear someone say? Yes, but then World War II would have broken out much sooner, as soon as the nations had recovered from their terrible losses. It is in order finally to put to rest such recurring nightmares of which Bosnia is a painful reminder that Maastricht is so important.

'*The European* . . . will continue to fight for a Europe for its people — not just its politicians', is the final clarion call of the editorial. At last I can agree up to a point. But first of all, dear *European*, find a substitute for politicians. And, even more difficult, find whole-hearted consent about anything, anywhere, at any time.

17 September, 1992

Irony in the Soul

It used to be a kind of sinister warning to those embarking on theatrical tours — beware of this or that audience; they have no sense of irony.

This was a fairly general truth in places either too rich or too small to need such a sense. I used to think that the United States was too large to be needing a dose of irony in its diet, whereas Monaco was too small to afford one.

Certainly, allusion was frequently lost in these places; more so in the USA than in Monaco, simply because, as far as audiences were concerned, the overwhelming proportion of those in Monte Carlo came from ten minutes away, over the border, whereas those in the vast spaces of the West were strictly on their own, with no sounding boards except the wailing prairie winds, and no example apart from the wagging fingers of parental piety and the illustrated bibles as altar pieces of the mind.

This has gradually changed as television and its wild variety of discordant images has forced new and often disturbing impressions on minds rendered flexible by inexperience. The result of all this, quite apart from a series of murders for reasons even the culpable fail to understand, and a spate of other behavioural quirks is, inevitably, an increase of both irony and scepticism.

The general quality of leadership has done nothing to allay this change of perceptions. Mr Ross Perot is a living symbol of the march of irony into the affairs of state, even if he retired in time to give absurdity its head in an election so long that it influences every moment until the following election.

Although local heroes are hailed by every trick in the growing arsenal of public relations, a degree of irony seeps through the cracks. The sight of Mr Reagan swimming gallantly for so long out of his depth, made buoyant only by the rubber duck of his talent as a great communicator, cannot have failed to make at least a few realize that he had precious little to communicate.

And now, with Mr Bush, the character has altered, but hardly improved. Even if the testimony of personal friends as to his like-ability is impressive, that will neither win nor lose elections. He gives those uninfluenced by his qualities as a man, golfing partner, or whatever, an impression akin to those irritating children who can never be wrong. His index finger stretched to the limit, he illustrates his points laboriously, as though talking to natives in some remote part of the planet who seem unwilling to accept beads as legal tender.

And, what he comes up with is frequently an idea which seems to have broken in on him like a thunderclap, but which practically everyone else has thought self-evident for years. The onlooker is therefore struck less by the originality of the thought, than by a question of why it has taken so long to penetrate, and how many grave miscalculations have led to its ultimate adoption as policy.

And as a background to the somewhat pallid confrontation of ideas, there is the usual quagmire of dirt raked up by researchers into the secret lives of the candidates, as though a moment of temptation in the 1960s had a vital bearing on fiscal policy today. Luckily, the avenues of sexuality have been exhausted by the grunting truffle-hunters, and they have now turned their attention to the military careers of the candidates.

In a television programme on CNN entitled 'Crossfire', dedicated, as its name indicates, to overstatement at its baldest, there was a recent comparison of the relative patriotism of Governor Clinton and Dan Quayle.

Pontificating over this bizarre evaluation was no less an authority than Ollie North, the virtuoso of the shredding machine. This beacon in the dark night of doubts declared that he knew many conscientious objectors, and had the highest regard for them, so long as it was their religious beliefs which led them to decline to fight on principle. This was very different, he suggested, to being willing to fight in some wars and not in others. The butt of the heavy handed nuance was of course, Governor Clinton, who was known to have been opposed to the war in Vietnam — an error of judgment which still produces its tragic echoes and aftershocks.

But Ollie evidently considers that orders are orders, be they in causes good or bad, and they are to be obeyed. And if there are still any doubts about this, he is, one seems to remember, a shining example of all that is creative in the interpretation of such orders.

Naturally, programmes like this are breeding grounds for the cocoon of irony, but irony in its most natural and unaffected form comes largely from places which have known the contradictions of history for a longer time. Take the contested territory of what was once Yugoslavia. According to the 'Quotes of the Week' column in *The European*, a Bosnian soldier is alleged to have said in Sarajevo, 'We call this peace — we only get a couple of hundred shells a day'.

Meanwhile, quite close as the missile flies, in the holiday resort of Sveti Stefan, Bobby Fischer created a sensation after his rival Boris Spassky had evened the score in their series of chess matches, by requesting that the entire audience be removed.

His reason? One of the onlookers had sneezed while he was about to make a move, thereby destroying his concentration and causing his defeat.

And yet, whereas the mind is wide open to the latest absurdity in the daily catalogue of contrasts, there do still occur events which bring a sparkle to the jaded eye, and sound like music to the languid ear. A delegation of factory chiefs from the Kuzbass region of Siberia turned up in Geneva, seeking the possibility of Swiss investments in their industries and a degree of technical collaboration.

Mr Sterligov, the spokesman for this richest coal mining region of Russia, which produces 40 per cent of all high grade coal, was very precise in his speech. He encouraged technical assistance and hoped for investment for mutual benefit, but declined finance as charity or gifts of food. He made it clear that if they were unable to feed themselves and lost control of their own solvency, they did not deserve to survive. This attitude went down well with the hard-headed Swiss.

The County of Durham is twinned with the Oblast [district] of Kostroma, north east of Moscow. A wonderful postcard from James Pollock, a student from Durham University who is spending his holidays there, together with other students, rebuilding the ancient monastery which was falling into disrepair. 'It is breathtakingly beautiful', he writes, and ends 'We have so much to learn.'

And only today, congratulations to an international school near Geneva, La Chataigneraie, whose students have helped materially in facilitating the work of a small foundation called Global Harmony. With no trace of paternalism or sense of superiority, this small organization teaches groups in Latin America and India to help themselves. Once the resulting team becomes independently efficient the instructors move away to help others towards self-reliance. The young people understand its aims, enjoy its novelty and assure its survival.

Irony is an amusing adjunct which makes many things of unbearable cruelty and harshness palatable. But what a relief, nevertheless, to record events which have no need of this condiment. And almost invariably, they involve the young, which is in itself a balm for the wounds of the daily grind.

24 September, 1992

Uneasy Ghosts

Like all ancient mansions with a modicum of self-respect, Europe has ghosts. It is to lay these ghosts to rest, to renew the mansion, to make it not only habitable but comfortable, that Europe is finally drifting towards union, or at least to the status of a decent and equitable condominium. The fears that this logical process seem to engender are very similar to the cobwebs which impair clarity of vision in the chaotic attic of this venerable building; breeding grounds for hearsay and superstition.

What is the nature of these ghosts, which begin wailing like well-protected cars in a parking lot, usually as a reaction to a false alarm? They vary from nation to nation, even from region to region. For instance, during Tito's later years Yugoslavia gave the appearance of a modern, cohesive state, with a well-established tourist industry, an opulent agriculture and growing sophistication in what was manufactured.

It was liberal by the standards of communism, and the borders were not sealed hermetically against the outer world and its influences. It was even, out of all proportion to its power, a considerable influence on the political scene as an instigator, together with Egypt and India, of the nonaligned nations, a formation which carried weight during the period of the Cold War.

Now Tito is dead, as is the Cold War, and suddenly, bereft of the tensions which gave it importance and a platform, Yugoslavia has diminished in stature, and this local drama has brought out the witchdoctors in their droves, conjuring up the ghosts from their uneasy rest. We know these particular ghosts well. They were no doubt healthy embryos during the four centuries of

113

Turkish occupation, growing in force as the ailing Ottoman Empire yielded to the inevitable by retrenching to that fraction of its erstwhile grazing ground now called Turkey, in Europe.

The races of the Balkans rediscovered their identities, and acquired monarchs in the market place. It was a gesture towards modernity at the time but it was not sufficient to bring them up to par. The ancient kingdom of Serbia found a dynasty of its own, as did the considerably smaller sister kingdom of Montenegro, governed by a monarch from the charmingly named Billiard palace in the old capital of Cetinje, which harboured the first billiard table on the Balkan peninsular — a cause of evident pride.

UNEASY GHOSTS

Croatia, Slovenia and Bosnia-Herzegovina were at that time part of another Empire which had not yet collapsed, that of Austria-Hungary. In the summer of 1914 as we all know, the heir to the Austrian throne was assassinated by a Serbian conspirator in Sarajevo. The ghosts rose like hackles in all parts of the continent and led the dance into the worst carnage history has ever recorded. The Treaty of Trianon which marked the end of hostilities for a while did little but shuffle the ghosts like cards, and let them find their own way back to their habitat.

In 1939 it all began again, with Poland as a pretext, but the Balkans were soon in the limelight once more. The Yugoslavia created by the Treaty was now redivided into separate entities by Hitler, with Fascist cronies in Croatia as savage participants in atrocities against the Serbs.

Finally, Tito and the Communists carried the day and created the Yugoslavia we thought we knew. When they had had their fling, and communism was generally discredited as being not only inhuman, but guilty of an even greater crime in a world not known for its sensitivity — that of gross inefficiency, the last remnants of Serbian party bosses took the only escape road — that leading to patriotism, and now trumpet nonsense about the need for ethnic cleansing, while having a go at the Croats for what they did to the Serbs half a century ago. The ghosts are having a field day as rarely before in their history, Sarajevo being an ideal place for them to vent their blood-thirsty nostalgia.

It is in the Balkans that the phantoms are at this moment at their most deafening; but let no one imagine that the rest of Europe is spared these presences. The illness is highly contagious, and we are all prone to its nefarious influence. The pound sterling has only to slip from its communal nest for angry fingers to be pointed at the German Bundesbank. Here it must be said that the press matches the markets themselves in nervousness, making mountains out of molehills with all the dogged application of those whose duty is seen to be the creation rather than the recording of news. John Major has only to make a characteristically precise yet ambiguous reference to Germany's fiscal policy — a seeming paradox, and yet such is his special gift — for sections of the press to scream that 'PM Slams Kohl', or some such elegance. If Kohl appears to retaliate in a carefully worded comment calculated to avoid controversy, the report will tend to be something like 'Bonn smears Britain'. Any gesture which artificially heightens tension can be characterized as an appeal for the ghosts to rise, and although capital for investment may be in short supply, and jobs may be lacking, there is never a shortage of ghosts.

These materialize in their platoons at the sound of a distant bugle or of a word spoken in anger. Even the Gulf War, that unfinished victory, was a cue for all the conditioned reflexes of recent history to be invoked.

On television, the uniformed lady stood before a piece of artillery which barked its message into the distance throughout her commentary, and she called out 'The guns behind me have joined the battle and they are British'. Here I turned off. The ghosts were too evident as they held up the text for her to read.

It is most interesting that in the recent French referendum the parts of the country to approve Maastricht were those close to borders or on the coast; in other words, those in contact with other nations and other traditions. Strasbourg, a city which is a hive of European activity and which has benefited materially from the connection, voted overwhelmingly for the Treaty.

It was the most cloistered central parts of the country which tended to vote against. The French and the Germans, with a hideous common history of spilt blood are the most successful in the difficult task of exterminating their ghosts as the parasites they are. Perhaps it was the sheer horror of their experience which made the reconciliation between de Gaulle and Adenauer a necessity. The rest of Europe is in urgent need of exorcism from this half-hidden blight, the plague of ghosts.

1 October, 1992

If this is Monday, it must be Mülheim . . .

The end of summer is not a matter of weather these days but of activity. The sudden old-fashioned peacefulness of the traditionally warmer period of the year is like a rediscovery of the past; the landscape passes at the speed of the languid walker, thoughts idle on the confines of the mind as do daydreams. Holidays are a vital reminder of what man was before human ingenuity invaded his sanctuary with endless distractions.

Then it all begins again, from the normality of the Middle Ages to the normality of today. There is no climatic barrier to cross, no discernible frontier between idleness and feverish activity. It may well be pelting with rain in September, or wonderfully balmy thereafter. Never mind, the good days are behind us, the better days ahead. We accelerate with the inevitability of an airliner on the tarmac.

I admit I cheated to make the break less brutal. My first stop on the way into orbit was Dublin, a place which, despite evidence of modernity, has conserved a luxury of time like a garrulous drinker at a well-worn bar.

The pretext for my visit was some anniversary or other; it was never clear which, nor does the knowledge matter or spoil the fun of a fine television talk show under the aegis of Gay Byrne. Ireland may not have the financial resources to supply the weekly adventures of an Irish detective in the sleezy part of Limerick or in the rainwashed docklands of Cobh. But when it comes to talk shows, she is the unparalleled queen of television. After all, have the Irish not been rehearsing their talk shows ever since the days of St Patrick? And Gay Byrne, with his pixie truculence and truffle-hunter's nostrils is the virtuoso of the gab, as well as being the Toscanini of the gab of others.

Josef Locke, of all people, sang some Irish ballads with a mixture of subtlety and wreckless fervour which held the attention to say the least. There was a stunning film about incidents of his life called 'Hear My Song', and abruptly to see the real legend before you was like being present when King Lear decided to give up the moor as too draughty and come indoors to sing the tunes carried by the wind during his wanderings. Then there were several comics, including one who painted an hysterical picture of an Ireland isolated by virtue of the fact that she was the only country to vote convincingly for Maastricht, with the terrible result that she was the only country condemned to live by its rules.

Finally in this galaxy, an appearance less jocular and less political than most, the ex-Prime Minister Charles Haughey, carrying an anniversary gift to the programme. This consisted of a stylized nest made of elm wood holding three wooden eggs, one made of elm, one of laburnum and one of some other wood. I cannot remember which: I had it explained to me too often.

Mr Haughey, whose haircut must be calculated to give him the look of a 12th-century friar with ideas of his own, carried the object as though he were the guardian of the Holy Grail, and explained that it was made of species of elm which is dying out, a slightly gloomy but very Irish note to strike on a joyous occasion. What is certain is that there was one less elm once the bowl was fashioned. From Ireland to Brittany, and a hotel which counted eighty steps to my room, the majority of them down, but a few of them up. Outside on an iron grille, it boasted a plaque announcing that it was a *Relais Gastronomique*. In answer to my breathless enquiry about the amount of further stairs leading to the restaurant, I was politely told that there was no restaurant. It was hard to believe I was not still in Ireland.

The reason for my being in Dinard was that this pleasant seaside town, perhaps envious of its larger sister down the coast, Deauville, with its famous festival of American films, had inaugurated a rather smaller festival of British films. There were Union Jacks everywhere and, as befits a function in a Celtic land, the inaugural ceremony took place at night on the beach in pouring rain.

Since *Lawrence of Arabia* was featured, some local horsemen galloped up and down the sand in Arab dress, but so far away from the spectators that they looked like galley slaves in some ghostly regatta.

The opening film was *Vice Versa*, which I wrote and directed in 1947. Despite my trepidation, it gave me quiet confidence in my future.

I shall remember Dinard for a wistful seascape, its steps and the warm-heartedness of the Mayor and the Festival authorities. Also for the best scallops I have ever eaten, at a minute restaurant called *Le Goeland*. The chef is an odd genius who hates publicity either for himself or his restaurant. I am sorry to break his trust. I do it piously like a tabloid in the public interest.

Next by private plane to Madrid in order to open the festivities marking the city's election as Europe's cultural capital of the year. I was to give two performances of my one-man show in English as an hors-d'oeuvre to an extensive cultural banquet. Madrid supplies its own jet lag. The opening night began at 10.30, which inevitably meant it was closer to 11.00. After the show there was an intimate dinner for some forty people. Lights out at 4.00 in the morning. I was surprised by the large proportion of the audience which spoke English, although when I attempted two numbers at the end of the show in Spanish, including my impression of a flamenco singer, pandemonium broke out, expressed in rhythmic cries of 'torero', I gathered afterwards that this is flattery at its most acute, although at the time I thought that, like Van Gogh, I might have to sacrifice an ear.

At dawn, after the second performance, into a plane for Mülheim-an-der-Ruhr, the capital of Germany's leather industry. Here, in a park exploding with greenery and flowers, and in the ferocious sunlight of an Indian summer most welcome after the bleak rain of Madrid, I spoke a so-called *laudatio* or *paean* in praise of Hans Dietrich Genscher, Germany's most consistent and imaginative Foreign Minister. Since he was the architect of German reunification, as well as being the first responsible western leader to understand the full ramifications of Gorbachev's and Shevardnadze's sincerity, it was not too difficult to find the right words, even in defective German.

And now? It is one day and a half later; I am in Room 322 of the Peninsular Hotel in Beverly Hills. It is 5.46am local time, 1.46pm in Europe, and I am finishing this article. Bush, Clinton and Perot never stop appearing on TV. With the sound turned down they look like over-actors in a dull, silent movie. And what will tomorrow bring? One thing — or rather ten things — at a time. Roll on summer.

8 October, 1992

Our Royal Heritage

It was the insistence of a German periodical that I express my views on the British relationship to their Royal Family that set me thinking about the attitudes towards royal families in general in this casual age.

One must, of course, understand that the British have a densely populated area at their disposal, and that as a consequence they have a truly national press which can penetrate into every nook and cranny of the Kingdom during the night. This entails circulations which are astronomic by most other standards. Over a million is no rarity. This entails, in its turn, a permanent fight for survival on a very high and dangerous level. It follows that a permanent titillation of the public sense of curiosity is a must for the maintenance of a necessary level of sales.

This warfare demands the requisite amount of sensationalism, and finds it with the greatest facility in the sheltered precincts of Buckingham Palace. No trick is too low, no innuendo too snide, too strident, too blatant to uphold the pious assertion that all this activity is due to an acute sense of responsibility towards that convenient abstraction, the public right to information.

The public right to mendacity, the public right to squalor, the public right to nonsense is never discussed, presumably because it is taken for granted and so well catered for that it is never in short supply.

What makes the British royals so vunerable to these assaults on their privacy to which they appear to have no right? Well, the attitude towards them is never clear, being a mixture of medieval deference and modern truculence. They are bowed to, curtsied

121

to, answered but never questioned and expected not to notice when, in violation of every unwritten law, they are insulted.

At the opening of Parliament, the Queen sits on a throne with an ungainly crown on her head, and reads a speech expressing the views of the Prime Minister as formulated by those who write his speeches.

Now, nobody ever thinks that she, as a highly intelligent and lucid person, may well hold opinions at total variance to what she is forced, by tradition, to say. It is known that the Prince of Wales is passionate about the future of architecture, that he has an artistic temperament expressing itself in words and water-colour, both of which are shyly allowed to see the light of day at times.

And yet the strictures of royalists and professional people are invariably loud and clear about any expression of human involve-ment in matters which concern us all. Professional people, espe-cially architects and town planners, should perhaps be a little more tolerant towards opinions not necessarily their own, because in the Royal Family they are dealing with people even more highly professional in their way than they themselves.

As for royalists and self-appointed arbiters of behaviour in exalted places, they are perhaps most to blame for the extraordi-nary maintenance of rituals which ensure that there are those, in this day and age, enslaved by the habits of centuries while exposed to the cat-calls of today.

King Juan Carlos has a much easier time of it, undoubtedly because the monarchy in Spain has been intermittent and he has therefore been able to make his own rules and adapt the ancient pomp of the Spanish court to the exigencies of our age. He gives the impression of being a far more modern royal than his British counterparts, being at all times accessible and not, to borrow a phrase from a famous trial, economical with his opinions. He has decided to be a man who happens to be a king rather than a king who happens to be a man.

And there is the nub of the question. There was never any doubt that the Scandinavian monarchs, who used to bicycle around their capitals were people like any other merely born to a higher saddle. They chatted to their neighbours when the lights were red, and tinkled their bells as signs they wished to overtake like any other street-trained citizens, and if they have now had to give the practice up, it is doubtless for the same

122

reason so many liberties have had to be surrendered; security.

Intrinsically however, they are the same servants to the habit of being cosy kings and queens. Britain is no longer quite sure where she stands in the matter, having exalted the function of royalty to that of demagogue status after many centuries of piled-on precedent in the not-so-distant backwash of the happy and glorious protocol of Queen Victoria.

Yet now she seeks to streamline the institution in order to seek a compromise with the turbulent electronic times we live in. It resists streamlining with the same inflexibility one of Queen Mary's fleet of Daimlers would have. Before Queen Victoria and the empire-builders, Britain already had her crises of the same nature, with for instance, Oliver Cromwell, whose place in history has always been a cause of embarrassment. He was certainly a man of destiny, ruling with a stern hand after he had caused the king to be beheaded — a degree of criticism of the institution to which none has aspired since. He was rewarded by a long road away from the centre of London and a small statue within the precinct of the parliament he discredited. He was denied a battleship despite the efforts of Churchill when First Sea Lord, who recognized greatness before he would admit to wrong-headedness.

The King was opposed to his choice for reasons of his own. After Cromwell, George IV was a most peculiar King, cursed with multiple gifts which is anathema to one who must pretend to be only half a person. He could imitate all around him and frequently did. His breakfasts often lasted five hours, only to be interrupted by lunch. He mixed champagne, port and hock with swigs of laudanum, and often ate a steak and two pigeons as a mid-morning snack, never disguising his love for Mrs Fitzherbert while the divorce from Queen Caroline took place in the House of Lords.

In case there are those who think that scandal about royalty is a new phenomenon the great caricaturist Gilray was less gross than Spitting Image but no less mordant. In only one way have we advanced: today royalty is an endangered species and may well be deficient on human rights under the Helsinki agreement.

15 October, 1992

The View from Vienna

To be in Vienna is to have a sidelong, and yet undistorted view of the world. The walls of the hotel room are of golden silk with a dim, floral motif, set into apertures in off-white wood. The curtains are as heavy as those in a novel by Sir Walter Scott, deserving a page of minute description each time they are referred to, and there is a portrait of an imperious lady in the court dress of the last century.

All this exudes an atmosphere of self-confidence in a past which has long since gone, both quaintly pleasant and slightly unnerving. On a white-and-gold commode, built cunningly by a modern carpenter to conform with the baroque atmosphere, there stands a very modern television set, so that, like living actors in an ancient theatre, the personalities of today can invade this silent backwater of glories past.

Ross Perot's unharmonious voice bites like acid through the echoes of Mozart, while President Bush stands glinting away, his querulous tones seeming to repond to distant pit signals. 'Attack his character now — it's your last chance', or 'let's have a bit of humility — admit your mistakes — not all of them for pete's sake', while Governor Clinton regales the spectator with what is deemed to be an infectious grin, not so very far removed from that of Stan Laurel.

Curiously enough, seen from an islet of stability, in which the noise of horses' hooves from the street would not surprise, these debates seem even more depressing than in a contemporary setting. It is as though the Wimbledon Championship is to be decided by three lucky losers from the qualifying rounds.

Mr Major does not escape the baroque treatment either. Walking backwards across a road, waving and weakening his arguments by afterthoughts until he reaches the sanctuary of his car; and Mr Heseltine reading his statement on second thoughts about pit closures like a punished schoolboy to the blustery heckling of the opposition.

Once the television set is turned off, and the ephemeral rush of events is over, the room reverts to its seemingly indestructible self. Vienna is an interesting city, in that it is a great survivor. The Turks have knocked at its gates, and Napoleon's troops made quite a habit of camping here, to the annoyance of Beethoven, among many others. The Russians were here after the last war, and it is one of the few places the Communists left voluntarily to its own devices.

Austria has always enjoyed prestige, even when enfeebled by defeat, and during the total occupation of the country by Hitler. It is here that the famous description of an impossible state of affairs was coined: 'the situation is desperate, but not serious'. The Congress of Vienna took place here, at the end of that sickness of Europe called the Napoleonic Wars. Austria, as one of the greatest sufferers from the years of conflict, was deemed worthy of hosting such a far-reaching conference, and even today the city is the home of one of the vital agencies of the United Nations, that governing atomic and nuclear energy. There are few cities in the world still redolent of an imperial past. Rome is one, as is Cairo, but for reasons rendered abstract by the passage of time. In Rome, as in Cairo, the surviving vestiges of empire are reduced to obstacles interfering with the free flow of modern traffic. An imperial atmosphere is felt in the high-strung air of Paris, where imperial is an attitude of mind, the grandeur to which Le General so untiringly referred, and which pertains not only to battle honours, but to furniture, to the senses, to taste in general. London, too, possesses an imperial personality, despite the disappearance of empires. There it evokes a certain stability, not to say immobility. Traditions linger even when they verge on the nonsensical. Blackrod tapping the door of Parliament three times after having had it shut symbolically in his face, as a permanent reminder of an incident most people have forgotten about or have never known, is typical of this abnormal respect for useless bits of history. But then, the British feeling for ghosts is friendly, even possessive. And they recognize eccentricity as an

125

ideal grazing ground for humour. The British enjoy a good laugh at their own expense, even if, at times, it is only to take the sting out of the laughter of foreigners.

Vienna is quite as imperial as the other cities mentioned; all the more remarkable in that, not only has the empire disappeared, but even some of the mother country — the South Tyrol, which now belongs to Italy as a reward for her having come into the First World War on the allied side. The Austro-Hungarian Empire used to include Hungary, Czechoslovakia, bits of Romania, Slovenia, Croatia, and Bosnia and Herzegovina. It was quite a lot to lose, and all of it in Europe. It was feared, with reason, that Vienna would prove too large a capital for such a diminished state to tolerate.

But what is the reality today? The British and French tend to behave as though their countries have not lost much in power or influence since the end of their empires. The Austrians do just the opposite. Time and again they emphasize the smallness of their country; not only politicians, but taxi drivers and hall porters. What are they trying to hide? Perhaps merely the fact that this is an eminently successful country — I beg its pardon, little country.

At a time when all others are wondering if recession is merely an overture to depression, Austria is doing remarkably well. Near the airport there is a gigantic oil refinery which refines a large proportion of Russian crude. They are into all manner of light but necessary manufacturing, including trucks, elevator equipment and the like. A long line of white-painted military vehicles suggested that they are involved in UN activities. This is so, agreed the taxi driver, but they have no activity in erstwhile Yugoslavia. This is understandable. If ever UN peacekeeping forces were deployed in Northern Ireland, British troops would hardly be welcome amongst them, for the same reason. 'Our past', explained the taxi driver. 'Our proximity to those people'.

The maid has just entered to remove the breakfast; she is Burmese. 'Life in Burma is hell,' she says 'but I managed to get out to one of the only six countries for which an exit visa is possible in Burma: Austria.' Of all the almost 200 countries, only six, one of them far away Austria! Is that not the best testimonial for the imperial mind which has learned to live with the times, and invest in humanity?

29 October, 1992

In the European Heartland

It is a relief of a kind to find oneself in the heart of Europe, where the word is accepted as a normal description of a reality instead of as a scarecrow for humans. Brussels is a charming city, with a personality which has survived the invasion of foreigners, described unpleasantly as Eurocrats, much in the way the meticulous bankers of Zurich are referred to as Gnomes.

All this is part of a campaign to create new myths as a basis for the prejudices of tomorrow. There is a general assumption that the so-called Eurocrats, who inhabit their building like bees in an enormous honeycomb, are avid for power, and possessed of an authority not theirs by right. That right, it is said, belongs to elected national parliaments. What it comes down to is the perfectly normal friction between ministries and their semi-confidential way of doing things, and the chaotic, more emotional style of those responsible to electorates and not to hierarchies.

Both are needed in a balanced democracy. In point of fact, it is because these structures lie in foreign territory that they are suspect to the traditionalists, not because they exist. The rub lies merely in the truth that in order to counter-balance the activities of the Eurocracy, it would require greater authority for the European Parliament, which entails, of course, less control over community matters by national parliaments. The European Parliament is, on the whole, a place of calm debate, perhaps because its decisions are not as far-reaching as they should be, and perhaps because the impacts are lessened by the filter of simultaneous translation. The stage is set in conformity with the majority of national parliaments in Europe, that is to say,

President of the Assembly, and so forth.

This arrangement tends to give focus to the discussion, as in a court of law, instead of the British formula, which ranges government and opposition on confrontational benches, like trenches in one of the great static battles of World War One.

Here they are free to shout and scream at each other, holding bunched order papers aloft like hand grenades, making such a noise that individual voices are never audible for long, and the speaker thumps her gavel like a metronome, exhorting the wayward scholars to remember their age with hopeless cries of 'order, order'.

A visitor from Mars with a penchant for democracy might well come to the conclusion that the more intelligent decisions are liable to emanate from the European Parliament than from a purely national one, especially in light of the condition of most of the countries represented by national parliaments, and the prestige of politicians in general in the communities. However, if we won't accept advice from foreigners, there's not much chance for the quiet Martian to make himself heard.

Be all that as it may, the majority of the so-called Eurocrats have revealed themselves to be intelligent and lucid creatures instead of the comic strip beavers which inhabit the imagination. In the smart restaurants very little French or Flemish is heard at lunchtime. There seemed to be a preponderance of Spanish and Japanese.

I entered one of the city's most reputed gastronomic shrines rather formally dressed, and alone, since my wife is in Paris. I was ushered to a small table. A waiter came up with a copy of the *Financial Times*. 'To while away the time, Monsieur Poirot?' he suggested. In a flash I realized I was home, in my own country, with rather tortuous roots planted by Dame Agatha Christie. In obedience to a conditioned reflex, I immediately assumed my best Belgian burlesque accent, and ruminated aloud. 'The *Financial Times*?' I mused, '*quel luxe!* It is long since I have had cause to peruse its pages. However, I will resist the temptation, since hunger is gnawing at my entrails. Nevertheless, it speaks highly for the class of the clientele that you should find it necessary to invest in a copy for the benefit of the solitary gourmet.' 'We only have the very best people here,' said the waiter, 'mainly from the Community.' I scowled, as I cast a febrile eye over the other diners. 'They are all potentially guilty,' I said confidentially, 'of crimes which are still waiting to be committed'. 'Have you just come from London?' the fellow asked. I pierced him with my eyes. 'As it happens, no,' I replied, 'although I admit that my reflection sounded as though I had just come from there.' I had no need for a newspaper. The other diners were sufficient diversion, once I remembered that Poirot derived his kicks in life by lip-reading at a range of up to 100 metres.

By this technique, I discerned several discordant notes in the conversations around me, but they resulted in no actual murders before I left the establishment. This is just as well, since nothing is further beneath my dignity than to be the actual witness of a crime. Gone is the sweet agony of deduction. Gone is the exercise of pure intelligence and the flattering gallery of amazed faces, usually furnished by the police.

'Is service included?' I asked the waiter as I prepared to leave. 'No monsieur,' he said, suddenly obsequious. 'How unfortunate for you, my friend', I snapped, as I remembered Poirot's stingy streak, and strode into the rain, as common as the market. I returned momentarily as myself, and left a gratuity.

Now I am in Holland. The weather is fine and cold. This is no longer the heart of Europe, but one of its arteries. There was no visible customs control between Holland and Belgium, or indeed between Belgium and Germany. It is all one country in all the ways that matter, and the racial troubles in Germany are regarded generally as distress within the human family, not as a symptom of some inherent fragility in the German character. Certainly the difficulties are well ventilated within Germany itself, which is quietly evolving a policy against what is clearly an international conspiracy of louts, eager on the dislocation of western self-confidence. The point is rarely made that Germany's record towards immigrants is second to none in Europe, and the many non-European faces in Brussels and Amsterdam reflect an exceptional tradition of hospitality to those in need.

Gypsies are the one sub-division of the human race who still evoke everything from misgiving to hostility, probably because of their independence from convention. A highly literate spokesman on television revealed the extent of their ostracism, and also the fact that there is no word for war in their language.

5 November, 1992

129

Pax Romana, Pax Americana

So it is over — the exaggeration, the impoliteness, the artifice. While it was still in progress, the candidates were steeped in the general air of mediocrity, and seemed more similar than they are. Only David Frost, who did his job beautifully, managed to prise them away from the images they had acquired during those unrevealing debates, where they were judged, as drama students might have been during auditions, for their performances rather than for the substance of their texts.

It was, of course, the victory of a younger generation — people who think of spontaneity as a virtue, or at least as a form of honesty, and who have no patience with the consensus seekers — those who try to appeal to some average statistical citizen while accommodating the wishes of influential pressure groups.

It was also a victory for the female sex, who may well be sick of watching the sanctity of life applied only to embryos and never to the living in a world grown callous by an excess of both cruelty and information. Children and the old, health and education, provide the most urgent problems today, and pious words about the wrong-headedness of those opposed to the Vietnam war have no profitable place in the list of tomorrow's priorities.

It was interesting to watch all the distant tumult from Rome, the hub of the ancient world. There is much in common between the *Pax Romana*, which stretched like an awful warning to miscreants over the map of the known world, and the *Pax Americana* today — a status quo imposed by a Security Council ready to be dragooned at any moment into the service of an international morality not uninfluenced by interests.

130

The openness of Roman society was a fitting example for Americans to follow. They have a relaxed attitude to life in general — 'take it easy' being an imprecation unlike that of any other civilization, with an emphasis on jogging, cosmetics, and physical well-being.

As the Roman Empire dragged slowly towards decadence, there was less insistence on the origins of its leaders, Dalmatians and Iberians being quite acceptable as long as they were imbued with a sense of the Roman way of life, a *modus vivendi* instantly recognizable by its practitioners. In America, too, there is less insistence on Protestant orthodoxy in its presidency. Already, in Kennedy, we have had a Catholic in the highest office in the land, and we have had Jews and blacks among the hopefuls.

It certainly will not be long before women make their presence felt in presidential races just as they have in the pulpits and before the altars of a changing world.

Human nature evolves so slowly that the changes are hardly perceptible at the best of times, imperceptible at others. Still, the new era in America, that most influential of societies, may well cast a light on some of the convulsions in other parts of the world.

Certainly, the drift to the Right, and the discrediting of the Left with the collapse of the socialist structures in the East was a tendency which had its repercussions the world over, but perhaps it has now come to a logical end; logical simply because, once it has reached its highest point, there is nowhere for the pendulum to go but back. With the end of the Bush era, the zany Right of the likes of Pat Buchanan, the redneck recruiting officers and holier-than-thou fundamentalists on faxing terms with deity, will assume a lower profile. The man in the street, too often these days the man in the gutter, will sense an unexpected flicker of hope in the dullness of his vision.

It may only remain a flicker, but it is better than no flicker. Once again, Rome and Washington have this in common. The pomp devoted to the celebration of the law is one of the really scandalous excesses of bad taste in our civilization. Take in the Palace of Justice in Rome, with its monstrous proportions, its orators in togas pleading lost causes from niches all the way round the building, allegorical groups engaged in indecipherable activities at every level, and on the roof a chariot with a blind-fold lady charioteer in charge of a quadriga of unmanageable horses ready to plunge into space — symbolic, one supposes, of the dangers of driving blindfold.

It is always a chastening thought that such elephantine piles (and every capital city has some paraphrase on this theme) are constructed merely to impress the lowest stratum of society, those criminals stupid enough to get caught. In fact, many of the finest minds in every nation are entirely devoted to defending or condemning poor cretins to months and years of incarceration or even death. But even here things are changing, in that with the coming of the supranational corporations, financial opportunity itself has become international as has conspiracy, the laundering of money and corruption itself.

The ex-Eastern bloc is invited to join the market economy at a time when an unprecedented number of fraudulent crimes has surfaced — a fine example for them to follow. The result is that a more educated type of person is now going to prison, which makes quite a change. Italian television has another similiarity with the vast grid of American networks, in that an endless chain of well-dressed men appears on the screen, taken into custody for irregularities in high places, swindles involving housing and public trust. The men struggle in and out of cars smaller than those to which they are accustomed, and are driven off to undisclosed destinations by the police, accompanied by lawyers with expressions both noncommittal and discreetly confident.

In Italy they have actually begun to seize documents at the most illustrious masonic lodges in search of links with organized crime. America has had a glut of sharepushers and the kind of Robin Hoods who rob the rich in order to keep the money themselves. Britain has had Maxwell and the Guinness saga, while France struggles with the miserable tale of doctors responsible for the diffusion of blood contaminated by the Aids virus. Prisons are filling up with smart people.

Reputable guides will grade prisons with stars for gastronomy and comfort. Prison governors will aquire reputations as hoteliers with colour televisions and mini-bars everywhere. Clients are advised to reserve their cells before they are caught.

But on the outer wall of my hotel there is a huge hammer and sickle, with the words, 'The struggle continues'. Mind the pendulum!

12 November, 1992

The Worst of all Worlds

The row over the General Agreement on Tariffs and Trade shows how interlocked our destinies are and to what extent we depend on the decisions of others. The American ultimatum, launched in the middle of an election campaign, looked more like an error of judgment than usual; the French over-reacted with panache and the rest of Europe showed a willingness for urgent talks after thousands of other urgent talks.

Meanwhile, angry farmers showered motorways with the fruits of the earth in sickening profusion. A Belgian striker, blocking a vital artery with his tractor, gave 'solidarity with our French brothers' as the reason for his strike. When pressed about the nature of the solidarity, he confessed he did not know.

In a period of increasing penury, in which politicians resemble weathermen who have predicted bright intervals during a day of unrelieved rain, there is a general sense of exasperation with matters which would scarcely raise an eyebrow in normal times.

Tempers are permanently frayed. Smiles of goodwill are strained and those who should know better are quick to take offence. Old prejudices reappear, while some examples of international collaboration work well. This grotesque return to the quagmire of ancient hostilities is as reprehensible as it is stupid.

Europe is unhappy because its conscience is not clear. There is a basic imbalance of priorities. If supranational corporations have become more powerful in certain parts of the world than elected governments, it is equally true that there exists a supranational element to terrorism, there being established links between malefactors such as the IRA, ETA and all manner of other weird factions killing innocents.

There is also an evident international link between the louts who desecrate Jewish tombs and attack immigrants, an activity too concerted to be put down to a chance local fever. All this can be attributed to a lack of European resolve and to the absence of Europe as a confirmed and powerful entity with a personality of its own, in addition to the personalities of its ingredients.

With such alacrity the heat was turned on Saddam Hussein at the outset of the Gulf War, under the pretext of an invasion of another member of the UN, and, of course, with the justification of danger to vital oil interests which conveniently coincided with the aggression on Kuwait. Even then, Europe lacked a cohesive enthusiasm. Only Britain and France sent small contingents for the sake of appearances so that the UN would not be synonymous with the US.

There is no such justification, apparently, for the permanent moral affront in what was Yugoslavia. This is hypocritically regarded as an internal matter within a country which no longer exists in its original form. How would the American colonists have felt if their struggle for independence had been treated by other nations as an exclusively British affair in the domain of internal jurisdiction?

Unfortunately, we have matured since those heady days of revolutionary fervour, and today's solution is to send in the UN, not in the way it was used in Iraq but in a strictly emasculated form, its troops unable to use their weaponry unless under direct attack.

This is clearly the worst of both worlds, while effete negotiations continue between frustrated diplomats on one hand, and on the other, liars and cheats with no interest in a solution other than that of force of arms. It is a reflection of the other anomaly — the US gun laws which decree that it is the right of every man to defend himself. The perpetrators of such a solution in the case of Bosnia-Herzegovina believe that the moral weight of the UN is sufficient to guarantee that the Blue Berets will not be carelessly attacked. In a sense they are right. The casualties are exclusively what they were before: men, women and children. This must be disastrous to the morale of the troops, permanently confronted by tragedy but unable to intervene.

Another ill-effect is that it has taught the Serbs how far they can go with their hideous policies — far enough for continued horror. Quite clearly the sanctions work less well than they could have in Iraq. Unicef, unable to pass through Customs with relief supplies, was reduced to buying them anew in Serbia — expensive but possible. That such an open wound is allowed to bleed untended and unsterilized is an insult to the sensibilities of the world, and a very real danger to the future of Europe.

This lack of resolve before a problem in our midst is an invitation for that madcap minority of mini-Valkyries to continue raiding refugee camps and sacred precincts, counting on the perplexity of the police at unusual situations.

Far be it from me to advocate the shedding of fresh blood as a solution to any problem, but European credulity is at stake on a broad front from Bosnia on one flank and Gatt on the other.

ISN'T IT WONDERFUL
To KNOW THAT WE'RE
ETHNICALLY CLEAN!

A surgical strike, so beloved of Schwarzkopf, against the Serbian artillery in the hills above Sarajevo would teach a sharp and salutory lesson, with the obvious rider that it could happen again if necessary.

Once and for all, we are not dealing with the internal problems of Yugoslavia. Slovenia and Croatia are already independent. Bosnia hopes to be, but is under attack from an aspiring Serbia and an only semi-quiescent Croatia. And there is Kosovo waiting in line for the tender graces of the Serbian warlords, to say nothing of Macedonia. If nothing is done now we will live to regret it.

How we react has a direct bearing on how we deal with hooligans who seek to exploit resentment against foreigners in times of unemployment and depression.

To close the borders is no dignified solution. For Europe to become a reality, we must be able to live with ourselves as well as with our brothers and sisters.

19 November, 1992

This Chameleon, Democracy

What is democracy? Whatever a dictionary may tell you, it is unlikely to give more than one definition of this much used, much abused word. Ancient Greece was the origin of both the word and the concept: the necessary privilege of personal choice.

A human being is a sacrosanct entity, not only capable of choice, but capable of taking full responsibility for that choice. Whenever conditions are such that this fundamental right cannot be exercised, other considerations creep in, as with the slogan of the French Revolution, and subsequently of France itself: *Liberté, Egalité, Fraternité.*

From the time of America's revolutionary wars, there has been competition about which country allows its people the greatest personal freedom. It is deeply ingrained in the Americans' psyche that they are the source of all modern democratic practice, even with all the adaptations the country has undergone during its expansion from the equivalent of a Third World state to the giant federal nation of today.

This immensity is traditionally fought over by two vaguely defined parties, in which the participation of a third element is not only discouraged, but rendered prohibitively expensive.

In that sense, politics is certainly more directly linked to money than is usual in less opulent societies, the saving grace being the freedom of movement of individual politicians permitted in the vague no-man's-land between the two factions. Lunatic ex-combatants with private armies, religious fanatics overheated by fire and brimstone, and Klansmen in their dunces'

137

hats are generally gathered round the right wing of the Republican Party. Hippies, flower people and deviates owe their allegiance to the left wing of the Democrats, but all the rest are strictly interchangeable, with the occasional exception of some maverick such as Ross Perot who seeks to create a new tradition of politics which doggedly resists every effort to spring into life.

Whether such a cumbersome system, understood only by a few Olympian observers, with its remote electoral college and results which have little direct bearing on the scores, really reflects the opinions of the voter is a matter of everlasting debate, as is everything else in a self-respecting democracy.

Britain has a different problem. Its democratic system is basic at best; primitive at worst. It is all very simple, based on a constitutional football match in which the government sits on one bench, the opposition on the other, with a few stray players from a smaller party permitted among the less promising reserves. The winner of the match takes all. The losers are left with nothing. Representation is not only never remotely proportional, but it has become a rule in recent years for the Conservatives to govern with a distinct minority of voices, which is not quite the democracy a purist would have dreamed of.

France attempts a rather more sophisticated solution, there being two layers to every election — the first seeing to it that the tiny parties are eliminated, like stains by a detergent, leaving the second layer for a realignment of the real contenders for a seat, which allows those who recklessly backed unelectable elements to transfer their allegiance to those with a chance of winning. It is certainly more democratic, and more expensive. Germany, having a federal system of great complication, the result of a division of the country into *Länder* of widely differing sizes and importance, has very little direct application to other systems.

The Italians, on the other hand, with meticulous attention to every shade of opinion, have rendered their country virtually ungovernable by a multiplicity of parties, sliding in and out of coalitions every time the government falls: very frequently, by other countries' standards.

There is a commission in session in Rome, trying to effect constitutional changes without recourse to a referendum. Onorevole Panella, the head of the small Radical Party, has been urging the commission to plump for the British form of democracy, at least for the Senate, whereas the French version seems favourite for the Parliament. He is an engaging orator. Accused of saying some destructive things about a friend of his in the chamber, he smiled charmingly and purred: 'I spared him the worst, out of friendship.' Will this sort of Machiavellian rejoinder still be possible if the Italian Senate is subject to the rigours of the House of Commons? Luckily there is no one potty enough to wish to emulate the House of Lords as an example to European democracy.

Naturally the Italians see only the virtues of the British system, and can only guess at the frustrations it engenders among people who never feel represented. I can only say that when I lived in Britain, and was therefore accorded the privilege of a voice, I never once voted for anyone who got into Parliament. For more than half a century my voice might as well not have existed. Which brings me to the point of this endless reassessment of our democracies. Are not political systems, like religions, basically a question of climate and geography?

The great Italian gift is the *combinazione*, the accommodation, by which the ungovernable is governed: the country is safest when there are no visible hands on the tiller of state. How will such an instinct for lightning reflexes cope with the scholastic discipline of an English school, so faithfully reflected in the youthful exuberance and occasional somnolence of Parliament? Everyone knows the British voting system to be unfair, yet it is believed, with relative sincerity, to be the best available.

Panella is evidently taken in by this myth, but what does he know of the British ability to live with injustice, to register a stiff upper lip when bearing its consequences, and of endless elegance in defeat? The luck of the game is a fatalistic British expression, redolent of that national masochism which believes that partaking in a test of strength is far more important than winning it.

The Italians don't believe that for a moment, and if they have any loyalty to their heritage, they will go on trying to win, in their own inimitable way, by complicating everything beyond the comprehension of others — including Onorevole Panella. Play to the whistle by all means, but try to be sure the whistle is on your side.

27 November 1992

Reflections on a Golden Statue

The Eternal City? Probably, more or less. It is certainly the city in which man has flirted with his own hoped-for immortality most outrageously and on widely differing levels of spiritual exaltation. On the one hand there is St Peter's, an overwhelming homage to a saint who was crucified upside down so as not to match the passion of Jesus Christ by seeming to imitate it. Certainly such a man would have things on his mind other than a future mausoleum.

On the other hand there was Nero, no great shakes as a spiritual authority, who built a statue of himself in gold a mere 70 metres high, and breathed a sigh of relief when it was unveiled, nibbled at the few bits of fingernail left over from the neurotic banquet and said, 'Now at last I can begin to live as a human being'.

It is extraordinary what some people have to get out of their systems before settling down to a life of dull normality. For how many anonymous strollers in the street would a 70-metre statue of themselves make all the difference between stress and serenity? Probably precious few in the over-populated crush of today; in which anonymity itself is the greatest threat to peace of mind; in which even certain crimes can be put down to a quest for identity.

It is far easier today for a fellow to commit a crapulous murder in order to command the scared respect of the tabloid newspaper reader than it is to construct a golden statue of himself 70 metres high. The cost would be prohibitive, to say nothing of building permits required today.

140

When the world was young, and relatively empty, people thought nothing of reaching for immortality in this uninhibited way.

However, a stroll through the Roman Forum emphasizes the vanity of such ambitions. Most of the columns designed to elevate lords and masters a little closer to heaven are still in place, even if the personalities they were built to support have vanished. The column which used to support the golden effigy of the Emperor Phocas is still intact and looks healthy for another 2000 years, but Phocas himself has disappeared. After all, this is Rome, in which things of commercial value, such as gold, tend to disappear, leaving things of little marketable worth, such as columns, intact. Phocas was melted down into cufflinks years ago, but his column remains.

How lucky and how lonely Lord Nelson is atop his column in London's Trafalgar Square, weathering storms he never had to face aboard the *Victory*! He has two great advantages. He is not golden and he is not in Rome. For those reasons he is still there for his span of immortality, a perch for gregarious pigeons and a point of reference for migrating birds.

But to revert to the city which so stoutly proclaims its eternity as a survivor of many disasters: Rome is no place for self-effacement or modesty. At least, whenever examples of these virtues appear in her story, it is always the kind of modesty one boasts about or the kind of self-effacement in which an empty space is more eloquent than a presence.

The great artists sometimes found little spaces for themselves or each other on their canvases to peep shyly through the gap in a hedge of bishops. But there is no ambiguity whatever about the presence, centre stage, of this or that pope, this or that king or emperor. Often even God the Father resembles someone one could have known. But as for Jesus, the image is practically a cliché, as though a face too full of character would, in some way, drag reverence down to the level of every day and imply a measure of disrespect.

But paintings, however flattering, however servile, never achieve the degree of self-glorification implicit in statues. Mind you, the really outstanding went beyond mere columns and merited arches. But they were never as personal as columns, resembling laundry lists of achievement in slowly perishable stone, as well as dramatizations in relief of highlights from lives dedicated to the misery and discomfiture of others — all of it seen through the eyes of workaday sculptors paid to be biased. The Romantic movement in painting and poetry was the first to use decay and disintegration as elements of beauty. And the byways of ancient Rome are evocative of shattered dreams and manhood spent in braggadocio, bluster and sudden death.

In the whiff of martyrdom and the drenching shower of celestial verities there is the sour after-taste of the venal and squalid in human nature. Rome is a recklessly human city, engaged simultaneously on all levels of mortal activity from the pious to the profane.

But times have changed. Cars are parked too deep in the narrow alleyways, scooters and motorbikes plugging every gap, and often there is a third car, temporarily blocking all passage in either direction. This third car dispenses yellow wheel clamps to the frozen mass of other vehicles.

Naturally there is an economy here, there being no need to clamp the cars nearest the pavement. Those which got there first, and which might even have a right to be there, cannot move in any case. In order to alleviate the congestion, ever more vehicles are diverted far from their destinations by an extraordinary number of policemen on foot, on motorbikes, in cars and on horseback changing chaos to confusion and back again at an immense cost to the patience and credulity of all.

The quick moods of the Forum are still there, but there are no giants left in the congealed mass of humanity which constitutes a modern city.

There are simply too many people for them to live without obedience to certain rules — some of them necessary, some of them idiotic, most of them both. The taste for columns is replaced by a taste for bank accounts, and a facade of democratic ambiguity is preferred to all opulent forms of glory which merely attract the attention of the city's fiscal authorities.

Even Rome by night has lost all trace of *la dolce vita*; the sleeping city being inhabited by vast armies of derelict cats. Seven of them sat in formation near a bus stop the other night. They looked as though they were waiting for a bus which would not now come till six in the morning.

The Colosseum is silent apart from the caterwauling of amatory cats. During the day they lie somnolent on the ruins, licking the wounds of the night and harbouring their mystery.

Not only men but also the lions of the arena, tamed by the rigours of survival in a regimented modern world, have seen their ambitions and rewards dwindle. Dustbins scraps have replaced the Christians' identity cards — the golden statues.

3 December, 1992

SIC TRANSIT

The Pressures of Evolution

In view of the stress to which we are subjected it is remarkable that we tend to outlive our medieval ancestors. They would not have known what to make of the word 'stress', unless it was used in the context of shipbuilding, architecture or the weaving of cloth. Consider the limits of their experience. For them, as for us, the sun was the most blinding of lights, but after this natural phenomenon there was nothing brighter than a fire in the hearth, a brazier and finally the candle.

The working day must have been considerably shorter and the eye only subjected to the strain of trying to work by flickering candlelight. An eight-minute-mile would have been considered the wildest dream, especially run barefoot or in pointed slippers, and fun and games were limited to maypoles for the poor and jousting for the rich.

If you had given a medieval man a modern car as a form of transport, he would have panicked at first, but if he had a fool-hardy nature, he might have coaxed it up to 30 kilometres per hour before crashing it into some obstacle, his reflexes being utterly unable to cope with the new frontiers of possibility, even after many lessons. As for attaining the legal speed limit, the crash would merely have come sooner.

The fastest thing he would ever be liable to see was a flight of arrows and perhaps a shooting star at night — but that was so unreal as to be merely decorative. In the realm of noise there was thunder and brass instruments in the cathedral, but nothing to match the total lack of silence we suffer from today. The sirens of fire brigades and of police, with their evil cadences, would have struck panic into the medieval hearts, and as for the sheer assault on the nerves practised by certain discotheques in which the volume is accompanied by psychedelic lighting, that stammering, stuttering abuse of the optic nerves, the poor friar of long ago would have believed himself prematurely in hell — a hell out of range of even Dante's imagination.

Television would have proved painful to him also. The succession of images being far too rapid for his comprehension. His eye would be attuned to static religious pictures, or conceivably to irreverent statuary high up on church towers depicting well-known clerical figures as gargoyles. But these objects allow themselves to be dwelt upon by the tranquil gazer.

His eye wandered at its own pace over the hidden detail, it was not bludgeoned into involuntary surrender by a mad montage of abstractions. In other words, we probably absorb more images in a day than our ancestor would have managed in a year, most of them ill-digested, lingering in the mind only as subliminal worry-beads recurring every now and then in the hopeless quest for interpretation.

There's no doubt about it, our bodies and our senses are pummelled in a way which would have been intolerable 600 years ago. And yet they surrendered to contagion and unhealthy living far more readily than we do. For that reason, perhaps, death was perceived as a necessary adjunct to life, and the concepts of heaven and of hell devoutly believed in lent a certain degree of morality to life and made of death an inevitability sooner rather than later.

Homeopathic medicine and herbalism were already far in advance of conventional medicine, but there was certainly a tendency towards fatalism which encouraged a gloomy acceptance of the worst at all times. There never seems to have been the almost hysterical flight before death which is apparent today, both in the sad bravery of those condemned by AIDS, and in the struggles of brilliant surgeons in the transplant of more and more unbelievable organs into the systems of the barely living.

Naturally, all this speaks highly for the resilience and the ingenuity of the human animal. In its contemporary form this animal is unwilling to accept the resignation of past times, and works overtime to negate the implacable rules of nature. There is no telling where, and if, the tendency will end. Certainly the increased activity of today has prolonged youth far into what was once considered advanced middle-age, and middle-age stretches far into what were thought of as the ultimate years of life span.

Exercise, the voluntary exhaustion of the human mechanism, is partly due to the speed of life, the need for lightning reactions in many fields of existence. The new obssession with diets and physical well-being, expressed in many ways from *cuisine minceur* to jogging and that orgy of hopping and skipping enjoying the typical pseudo-scientific name of aerobics, is a valid reflection of the preoccupations of today.

MONK ILLUMINATING A LETTER
IN THE MIDDLE AGES

And what lies ahead? Certain hand-picked individuals have already been introduced to the challenge of weightlessness, and this may eventually be a more general requirement as the inhabitants of the earth emigrate from the planet in search of pristine verities.

Many readers will still vividly remember Roger Bannister's cracking of the four-minute-mile. Nowadays, some runners, unable to qualify for the Olympics can manage this on occasions, and even that briefest of distances, the 100 metres, is under permanent assault, and inch by inch Bubka vaults higher and higher, whetting the appetites of avid youths now still at school.

These are all marks of human evolution, as are the development of sports equipment and other scientific aids to make the unbelievable possible. And yet there must be limits to the speed of human reaction. It is a wonderful irony that speeds on the stratosphere are such that total immobility sets in, enabling astronauts to climb out into space and disentangle crossed wires. Nearer home it must be that the speed of a fighter-pilot's reactions are somewhere closer to the present outskirts of possibility. The accidents involving formation flyers and individual war planes suggest that the border between daring and foolhardiness is, at present, just too vague to chance. Human beings are under enormous pressure not only from the stunning acceleration of technical development, but also from a gathering nostalgia for a past which seems so clear, so natural and so untroubled.

Is this so? How would you enjoy having a toothache in the 12th century? The dentist always came with a drummer to drown the patient's cries. There's a lot to be said for the times we live in, especially once discotheques are not compulsory.

17 December, 1992

Ode to Travel

Ah! The joys of modern travel in a season of goodwill, silver garlands already in many aircraft to remind you that the carollers are tuning up and that Father Christmas is practising deep breaths for his descent down all those chimneys simultaneously.

These garlands shudder in every mild airpocket as a tiny reminder of the fallibility of man and of the impermanent nature of his institution. The hint is there to be taken. Only the other day, I had a relatively uncomplicated flight from Frankfurt to Newcastle, with a brief stopover at Amsterdam. On paper this looked very comfortable, a departure at 5.20 in the afternoon and arrival at Newcastle exactly two hours later local time, with a relaxed dinner after the short motor ride to Durham, ready for a good night's sleep prior to the University graduation ceremonies the next morning. I left full of optimism. The comfort of the Lufthansa plane lulled me into a feeling of serenity only slightly offset by the time we spent on the tarmac, waiting for either a clearance from Air Traffic Control or else tardy passengers. With a delay of a mere 20 minutes, it seemed slightly hysterical to ask for reasons. Instead I glanced frequently at my watch and was rewarded by a marzipan reindeer, like a child who kept dropping his toys out of the pram. The flight itself was normal, and we landed at Amsterdam after the usual meandering over the outskirts of the city due to overcrowded air space. In Amsterdam, I found I had a long walk down endless corridors to reach the gate where the British aircraft was kindly awaiting my arrival.

148

However, I had been warned in Frankfurt that they were unable to issue a boarding pass for a place as exotic as Newcastle and that I would have to procure one in Amsterdam. I found an inquiry desk with queues of agitated passengers before both of the girls on duty. I chose the shorter queue which is often a mistake under such circumstances, since the traveller who has actually made it to the desk is too often a veiled lady speaking nothing but a local dialect, who wants to know how to get to Mogadishu on a ticket issued in Bahrain which expired yesterday.

When eventually I reached the front of the line, the large blonde girl told me, after consulting a computer which had to be hit once or twice to cough up its secrets, that the British plane had left, that there were no further flights to Newcastle and that in any case I was at the wrong counter, encouraging me to go to another one where I could already discern a long queue.

Of all airports Amsterdam is the one where seasonal goodwill is perhaps put to its hardest test. When at last it was my turn at the new counter, the small oriental lady confirmed that the British plane had left, and asked me by what means I had reached Amsterdam. I told her I had come by Lufthansa. She had to go to her bag, which was hanging from the back of a chair, in order to fetch a bundle of papers which seemed to contain some vital telephone numbers. She found what she wanted with some difficulty and dialled a number. After three attempts she got an answer, then replaced the receiver and looked at me accusingly, declaring that SAS had not had a landing for an hour. I said I had come by Lufthansa. She became irritated and consulted her papers at length. Having found what she wanted she tried again for an eternity before replacing the telephone once more and telling me that Lufthansa had gone home.

'I don't blame them,' I said. She fixed me with her glowing eyes. 'At all events it's their responsibility,' she said.

I began to feel my hackles rise. 'I don't give a hoot whose responsibility it is; I want to get to Newcastle!' I cried, more than robustly.

'To where?' she asked incredulously, her face screwed up into a ball of effort.

'Newcastle,' I enunciated ferociously.

She consulted her computer. 'Is it in Europe?' she asked eventually. 'Or Teesside if you can't manage Newcastle,' I pleaded.

Her face suddenly lit up. 'New Castle,' she said in two words, and went on, 'the plane has been delayed. It is still at the gate if you run — but for that you need a boarding card and I can't issue them. You must go there,' and she pointed towards the desk I had come from where there was, as always, a long queue before both girls.

I ran to the gates without a boarding card, which was an academic gesture since there was no sign of the plane and the gate had evidently been dark for a long time.

At the next gate, however, there was a British Midland plane about to leave. I threw myself on their mercy. The plane was off to Glasgow, and I could see myself, exhausted in the back of a rented car on the way to Durham, trying with my failing strength to penetrate the jovial brogue of the driver.

The British Midland official interrupted my reverie saying that they had another plane at another distant gate, just about to take off for London. If I hurried. . . . They were marvellous, arranging a connection in London for Newcastle by another British carrier; and shepherding me onto their London flight, into which I staggered with a feeling of guilt that I had held everyone up.

I need not have bothered, since we waited for one or two others. That, and the holding pattern over London, meant that the Newcastle connection had evaporated by the time we arrived at Heathrow, the other British carrier proving as unhelpful as British Midland were miraculous. Having taken one look at me in Amsterdam, they had a wheelchair waiting in London and rushed me at the speed of light onto their last plane for Teesside which they held for me. The journey to Durham took about as long as a journey to New York but my bags were not as fortunate. I recaptured them after lunch the next day. The hold-up was not the Customs but the police, who considered them to be unaccompanied and therefore suspect.

I pointed out that my name was not written U apostrophe, and that with my kind of schedule and courtesy of Amsterdam I would physically not have time to do odd jobs for the IRA on the side. Under the impressive medieval robes I wore in order to award Sir Leon Brittan his Doctorate of Civil Laws *honoris causa* there lingered yesterday's shirt, but I flatter myself that I behaved as though it were fresh.

Now I really am in New York, having enjoyed a perfectly uneventful trip during which I slept a great deal. I'm therefore wide awake at four o'clock in the morning.

From my high window I can see Christmas decorations in the shops. May peace and goodwill invade every walk of life, every holding pattern in the sky and above all every so-called information counter at Schiphol Airport, Amsterdam.

23 December, 1992

Enslaved by the Royal Muzzle

In a warm-hearted gesture of admiration and of European solidarity, the French Academy of Political and Moral Sciences recently installed Prince Charles as an Associate Member, for his work as a late 20th-century man and an avowed European.

And he remains that, in spite of the latest bombshell, the sad failure of his marriage, and the fact that, according to some people, there is nothing left for the Royal Family to do right.

A report in *The Times* said that the Prince opened his speech of inauguration at the Academy defensively, saying that he had been warned not to mention the General Agreement on Tariffs and Trade (Gatt), Maastricht or sheep. He then proceeded to do so, if obliquely, to the consternation of MPs on both sides of the political divide. I congratulate him. Some time ago I wrote that he suffers the worst possible fate for a man in his endlessly equivocable position — that of possessing an acute intelligence and of being talented.

First of all, who were the people who issued the strictures about what he could and could not say? In the times of absolute monarchy — not the diluted form practised today — such people would probably have met an unpleasant end.

Peter the Great, another talented man who indulged his talents to the full, would no doubt have garrotted such advisers with their own beards. Peter the Great manufactured naval instruments in his own workshop, found a job in a Dutch shipyard disguised as a labourer, and was absent from his empire for months on end while he learned the trades which fascinated him. Nobody dared to tell him what not to say to his fellow men.

Even Louis XVI, the mildest of kings, was able to make and repair watches to his heart's content in the quiet of his palace, where, poor misguided monarch, he even gave technical advice to Doctor Guillotin, the father of the guillotine, suggesting that the original straight blade would cut more effectively if slanted.

There is no record of his last thought, but it may well have been: 'It works!'

Frederick the Great wrote innumerable works for chamber ensemble and flute. Nothing undiplomatic was ever discovered in them. Not so much as an anti-Austrian note.

But now back to our muddle-headed times, stretched between memories of what monarchy once entailed and the informality of the age. Prince Charles is allowed the indulgence of some pleasantly old-fashioned watercolours, pastoral landscapes which are familiar to him. These are even shown in public.

And yet, one feels that if he began painting slums or derelicts asleep on pavements or even detailed architectural sketches, the mysterious authorities with an index of unpaintable subjects would soon make their appearance. He would be warned about the delineation of distressing or disloyal images such as the French Embassy, the French end of the Channel Tunnel, or other such inflammatory matters.

In case it be thought that my implicit accusation of anti-French bias is excessive, may I revert, for a moment, to that reliable newspaper *The Times*. Its article on the subject begins as follows: 'Ignoring the official line of his government and the gut feeling of his compatriots, the Prince of Wales yesterday offered his philosophical support to French farmers. He was speaking in Paris surrounded by Frenchmen and accepting a French honour.' And, horror of horrors, the article says later on that he spoke in fluent, if slightly accented, French.

'Slightly accented' is the mitigating circumstance. Without that, the feeling of betrayal would have been overwhelming — that and the fact that the support offered by the Prince was philosophical and never for one moment polemical.

As always, he was speaking of values and the practically voluptuous feelings which the French apply to their farming, a logical adjunct to their sense of the joys of the table and the infinite subtleties of the palate.

American and even British farmers may, on occasion, be just as passionate, but never for the deeply personal reasons of the French. Not only the French, but the civilized world, would be irrevocably impoverished if these values were to disappear under the assault of the statisticians and the wholesalers. That the Prince should be sensitive to this situation speaks highly for his maturity and his culture, and proves his worth to the Academy of Political and Moral Sciences, an incongruous title redolent of ideals rather than reality.

It is a relief to know that, as a first step to total emancipation, the Prince may, from now on, speak his mind freely in slightly accented French under the cupola. And in that sanctuary, what he says is none of the business of the government, the MPs on both sides of the political divide or, indeed, of the unproven gut feeling of the population.

In this connection it is good to know that the National Farmers' Union in Britain expressed considerable sympathy with the French farmers' fears about the impact of the Gatt settlement, and added fears of its own about the effect of British agricultural policy on the fabric of rural life.

The pursuit of democracy is relentless today. Efforts are consistently made to push democracy down the throats of those with neither experience of it nor, as yet, any feeling for it. Is it not a contradiction that in such times there are still degrees of slavery not merely among the extremely poor, but among the highly placed? Poverty is, by definition, a form of slavery but so, in some circumstances, are rank and public exposure. As for the Prince of Wales, the time in history has come for him to enjoy that freedom which is the birthright of every individual.

In case it be argued that historic precedents stretching back to the dawn of constitutional monarchy make it difficult to shed the evident anomalies of royalty so precipitately, I would point out that most of the stuffiness dates from Queen Victoria and her determination not to be amused.

Before her, scions like the Prince Regent made sure of their own liberties. But Queen Victoria reigned for so long that concepts of what was done and what was not done became as indelible as the rules of a game and are rarely questioned to this day. It is time for Britain to emancipate its last slave and not leave it all to Europe.

31 December, 1992

Virtue and Vice

It is logical, to my mind, to take one's holidays in winter. Summer is usually a wonderful time to rediscover one's own home. Everyone else is away, jockeying for position on some distant beach or vantage place on the landscape, and more important, they all think you must be doing the same as they.

The phone is blissfully quiet, and even the fax machine spews out its messages grudgingly. In winter they all think you must have your nose to the grindstone in the northern gloom. The telephone rings with the insistence of a guard-dog's barking, and the boa constrictor of the fax messages makes it impossible to enter the room upon returning, the saving grace being that the machine eventually runs out of paper during one's absence.

To leave home where the visibility is practically nil, to rise above the clouds to a layer of the earth's atmosphere blessed with almost permanent sunlight, is a foretaste of the sudden shock many hours later of emerging into the intensive heat of the tropics, still wearing the coat and tie belonging to the other parts of the world.

It is dressed like this that one faces the customs. True to the Orient, the tendency to smile is never absent as a sign of Buddhist composure and serenity, but there are times when the smile becomes enigmatic rather than open, for instance when invited to enter an office by one official, only to have the superior official make the most peremptory gesture requiring the presence of your documents, but not of your person. The inferior official immediately invites you to get out, the smile frozen on his face, but meaningless.

All this is a reminder of an implacable hierarchy which exists outside the hotel, and which a foreigner may study as a phenomenon, but not too closely if he wishes his vacation to do him some good.

Thailand is a place of multiple attractions as a complete change of pace. Endlessly tolerant on the surface, it has been a mecca for the over-sexed of every tendency. It is nothing exceptional to run into an embittered European millionaire with a running sore of marital problems, searching in the evening of his life for a teenaged Thai to do his bidding without coherent question, or else an Italian restaurateur from the north of England, or a man who once cut your hair in Stuttgart, or yet a dress designer from Rome, now seen in their true colours in the company of local youths, giggling at nothing much in sheer unadulterated elation.

It is natural that in this epoch of AIDS such permissiveness awakens concern, and is even surprising considering the rigour of the social pattern beneath the surface.

The language, for instance, is of extreme complication with a singular paucity of sounds, which entails eight different musical possibilities for each sound to express other meaning, compared to only four in Chinese. Also men and women speak differently according to their sex and not owing to the sex attributed to objects they are describing. This impenetrable barrier to immediate understanding does little to assist one in decoding a social structure full of unwritten rules and unquestioning acceptance.

The army seems to have a life of its own, with ambitions which appear to be political rather than purely military, or at least a dangerous mixture of the two. Within living memory, an insurrection of the military was put down by the unlikely intervention of the boy scouts, who took over traffic control and other civic functions regardless of the danger, and shamed the soldiery into an abandonment of their goals.

Lord Baden Powell can hardly have envisaged such a contingency when he coined his celebrated motto, *Be Prepared*. More recently one remembers a tragic popular riot suppressed by the army with many casualties, culminating in that extraordinary pacification ceremony by the King, seated on his throne while leading generals and political bosses crawled towards him on all fours.

It is a little beyond one's comprehension to be in a land in

157

which the divine right of kings still operates as a practical measure, even more exceptional in that this divine right is held by a monarch with great simplicity of spirit, who never for a moment abuses this right. A composer of tuneful music played by orchestras on festive occasions, he also interests himself in the technical side of agriculture, his experimental farm placing its researchers at the service of the people. His studious, bespectacled appearance cannot help but remind one of King Baudouin of the Belgians, who has a similar outlook on his duty.

Naturally, with such a paragon of kingly virtues on the throne, and such unequalled power invested in one person, it sets off speculation about what occurs when he is no longer there. As in all controlled and censored societies, rumours are rife and there are widely differing views about what will inevitably occur.

The inescapable fact is, however, that so much power invested in a single individual requires exceptional qualities of character and that these are not always forthcoming. Nero and Caligula both tried a little too hard to acquire them.

Meanwhile, the sea water is translucent and waveless, the sand pure powder and as one floats on this exquisite buoyancy in the ultimate gesture of physical relaxation, one can sense the presence of the sun, flame-red beyond closed eyelids. The utter inertia could go on forever. The weariness of body and soul drain away and even breathing is a rediscovered pleasure.

Last year at this time the hotel was teeming with military, far too many of them not to get in each other's way. The occasion was a state visit of the President of Laos, gravely stricken with diabetes, on his way to treatment in Bangkok. They carried him up to the Mirador of the hotel to enjoy the panorama of the bay. Although blind, he confessed himself well satisfied with the view. He died two months ago. Today there is not a soldier in sight, just waiters of elaborate courtesy, at least one of whom has just come out of a yearly retreat in a Buddhist monastery. His viewpoint is much more characteristic and profound than those of the soldiery, and his insight into the essential sense of values in Thailand is nobly credible after the smiles of officials, unconfirmed by their gestures or the expression of their eyes.

The waiter has developed what he was born with, the officials have merely copied others.

7 January, 1993

158

Good Guys and Bad

The battle lines are drawn up, and their composition is clear. As throughout history, there are the good guys and the bad guys; the light-coloured stetson and the dark, the suits of armour which reassure and those which terrify, the banners with symbols of life and those with symbols of death. And as throughout history, the good guys aren't entirely good and the bad ones aren't entirely bad.

Too many of them turn out to be grey when they bury the victims of a conflict; but then, with the passage of time, a second degree of forgetfulness sets in, and the winners miraculously recover their look of innocence, while the defeated sink back into an image of darkness and guilt. But that is for the history books, for the edification of the young, who will have to live through it all again when they are old enough to misunderstand. Or will they?

The good guys today seem to suggest that the human race must have reached its puberty at last, after all these centuries of painful ascent into a breaking dawn of intelligence, the great adventure of leaving primeval bogs in order to walk on two legs, and think with separate minds, and speak with many tongues.

As the world fills to a breaking point, standing room only threatens in many places; surely that is a sign as clear as any can be that the time has come not only to think of ourselves, but perforce to think of others. Our personal survival is now equated with the survival of the planet. We can no longer, as in some world conferences, exclude discussions on the population explosion out of deference to dainty religious considerations dating from when the world was young and empty.

No subject can be taboo any more. Everything, from AIDS and the emerging scourges of our overcrowded world, to the motivation of murderers, is subject for necessary ventilation and discussion. The need seems urgent at a time when values are changing under pressure of events, and the necessity for new thinking under the challenging realities of today and tomorrow is painfully evident. So much for the good guys, and the halo of enlightenment which illuminates their stetsons.

Now what of the bad guys? They come in all sorts of grotesque shapes, from Somalian war-lords, blaming outsiders for being unable to understand a rural underworld they can't understand themselves, Chicago ganglands without buildings or black sedans; Serbian bosses, who look as though they are as handy with the hairdryer as with the trench mortar, to the extent that they can't tell the difference any more. That's what ethnic cleansing does for a guy. Then there are the ethnically clean, the skinheads who dispense not only with hair but with brains as well, and who find physical well-being in fire-bombing the houses of the living and desecrating the homes of the dead.

Such people are joined in their recreation by fun-loving creatures like the Khmer Rouge and all those who believe that terrorism can be dignified by political pretension, and that one arbitrary explosion is very different from another one. The fact that innocents are killed in both makes no difference to them. Their bomb was the good one.

Naturally, this sudden convulsion of violence in many parts of the world is a reaction against the tendency of the good guys to bury the hatchets of the past and find a new code of human behaviour based on order and mutual respect. Faced by such an alarming provocation chaos must have its last fling, its macho self-indulgence. And we are only drawing attention to the most militant outburst of the bad guys, the activity of their patrols. Behind these outriders lies the main body of their army, high principled, addicted to tradition, as noble as they are unimaginative and often embarrassed to be confused in battle with the more unscrupulous elements of their own thinking. An acceptance of inherited values, and a continued application of outmoded structures to rapidly changing conditions is a hallmark of this army.

They are people who often know the second verses of national anthems, who haunt old comrades' reunions in order to delve for the comfort of human companionship into the past, who are voluntarily old before their time, out of feelings of security. To them, their world is as close to perfection as it will ever be. Why stir up a potential hornets' nest by searching for an improvement which might well turn out to be worse than what is already there? As they consistently reiterate, the trouble is that man is never content with his lot. And where acceptance is the order of the day, the words discipline and obedience are never far away, and nor is prejudice.

Compared to this general attitude, the good guys may well appear holier than thou as opposed to holy as the next man. The penalty of awareness is a general dissatisfaction with things as they are, and on the plain of the relationship between brothers and sisters of various loyalties and diverse creeds, this attitude may well appear pretentious.

Never mind, the good guys must risk giving this impression if they are to be true to their belief that all is not perfect. And they are working on some secret weapons. For instance, a concept which is very much in the air at this time is an International Criminal Court. Multi-national corporations are today's phenomena, spreading their authority even over conventionally assessed values, such as the relations between northern affluence and southern deprivation. It follows that crime has also gone international, where it cannot be pursued with much consistency. From there to the creation of Interpol is only logical, and now we wait patiently for inter-justice, an internationally accepted code whereby revolting theories like 'ethnic cleansing', or organized rape as a weapon of war can be condemned at once, and be prosecuted. It is obvious that, despite the efforts of the moderately bad guys to jealously preserve national parliaments, national courts of law and national armed forces as the highest levels of authority, requires time-consuming accommodations between nations when joint action is deemed urgent. This solution presents too many loopholes for organized commerce or organized crime to function without surveillance.

A unified currency in Europe is desirable, if for no other reason than that it entails the elimination of speculators, those highly volatile profiteers from the gusts of trade-wind in the market, and by the same token, an International Criminal Court is becoming essential owing to the global nature of business, both normal and criminal.

Equally global are the threats to our ecology, owing this time to man's ignorance and venality rather than to his ingenuity. A global agency for the protection of the environment is an equally urgent need.

Let the bads guys do their worst. As for the others, have faith, and keep your stetsons lit from within.

14 January, 1993

AN ETHNIC
CLEANSER

Ghosts Run Riot Once Again

It was to be foreseen with trepidation, then viewed with alarm, and finally with a deep disgust. The unwillingness of Europe to rise to even the most innocuous occasion is a signal for the ghosts of the old continent to run riot, like unruly children in an unattended classroom. The historical moments have passed unnoticed, the writing on the wall unread.

Despite the evident disasters of the past, Europe, this most powerful of continents by virtue of its influence, has preferred to dwell on the illusory glories of the past rather than to recognize the unique opportunity presented by a virtual rebirth.

We rely more on conditioned reflexes handed down as an inheritance from a bellicose history than on our intelligence. It is nothing short of tragic. Let us, at least, in the quiet backwater of a newspaper column, dare to look certain truths in the face.

Europe is responsible for the two greatest wars in history, both of which can be seen as attempted suicides which mercifully failed. Europe is responsible not only for Hitler and Mussolini, but, even more unfortunately, for the obedience these two creatures so readily commanded. It is fashionable, especially in schoolbooks and other sources of prejudice, to attribute the outbreak of the First World War to Prussian militarism.

To believe this as bald fact is to ignore that Prussian militarism was incited into maximum efficiency by French militarism, when that other self-indulgent vanity case, Napoleon, marched and counter-marched over the face of Germany, forcing independent German states into alliances with each other. And Napoleon himself came into being in the aftermath of the French Revolution, which saw the birth of high ideals such as liberty, equality and fraternity, and also witnessed their inevitable betrayal.

There was, alas, another reason for the First World War, and that was, quite simply, that there was no unknown world left to discover. Before that, European powers had tended to take their quarrels to far-away places, so that at least the Continent was spared the ravages of battle. But when the colonial adventure was over, the percussion section of the European orchestra was still exclusively composed of rattling sabres with nowhere to go.

Fairer, therefore, to attribute the almost negligent outbreak of hostilities to the habit of militarism and its attendant bluster at all points of the compass, not forgetting Serbian militarism and a predilection for plotting in that part of the world.

Now, after the laborious spadework of Jean Monnet and other apostles of common sense, Europe is on the point of being credited with its own identity at last, a rich amalgam of the diverse identities that make it up, and all the richer for it.

The most difficult, and what must once have seemed unthinkable, has already been done, and that is the Franco-German rapprochement, which inevitably awakens the suspicions of the British, nurtured on the conciliatory luxury of a balance of power.

But suddenly, there is no power to balance. Despite this detail, all seemed ready for the next step forward, the next demonstration of courage and imagination.

Unfortunately, a recession struck at the very moment that we were eager to demonstrate to those recovering from decades of dictatorship the advantages of a free-market economy. The moment could hardly have been more badly chosen. Our disarray became contagious and the Danes upset the apple cart by voting against the Maastricht Treaty.

This act gave encouragement to the retrogressive elements in all our societies who find mental solace in the bad old ways of selfishness and its meagre rewards. The fact that the Irish approved Maastricht passed unnoticed. The narrowness of the French approval was cited as an example of how confused Europe's volition is.

Still, John Major clearly sees all the advantages, and demonstrates his own form of stubbornness, like a terrier with a bone. The Danes are reconsidering. The future, as always, could go any way. Meanwhile, the recession goes on and on, with its attendant bankruptcies and human dramas. Even Japan is cruelly arrested in its rampancy, and Germany, that paragon of quiet industrial virtues, is compelled to reconsider its housekeeping budget.

Sensing a lack of European resolve, the dark forces of yesterday's chaos strike close to home. Yugoslavia, one of the proud fruits of the treaty-making at the end of the First World War, begins to disintegrate.

Ferocious and inhuman fighting breaks out between Serbia and Croatia, between Orthodoxy and Catholicism, between the Cyrillic and the Roman alphabets, and finally between speakers of the same language. Germany, surprisingly, leads the way to making disintegration inevitable by recognizing Croatia and Slovenia as independent republics; a reversion to historical policies which include, ironically, that of the Nazis. A non-combatant peacekeeping force is deployed in parts of Croatia by the United Nations, with the result that fighting spreads to Bosnia and Muslims are suddenly involved. Now protracted peace talks are reaching their culmination under the joint chairmanship of Cyrus Vance, for the UN, and Lord Owen, representing the European Community.

These talks have produced innumerable ceasefires, always broken before the ink is dry, and the Bosnian deputy prime minister is dragged from the protection of his armoured car and killed by Serbian troops. Is there really a chance of peace this time round? Lord Owen says the Serbs will not be inclined to stand by any treaty if they feel that world opinion is against them. One had not thought them capable of such sensitivity. But wait a minute — even that situation has deteriorated thanks to Europe's inability to express its revulsion in a loud voice.

The Russian conservatives who are such a thorn in Yeltsin's side have found a ready-made alternative in old-fashioned jingoism. These people, provoked in their self-importance by the pinpricks of the Baltic and Central Asia, have risen to the defence of their Serbian 'brothers' as part of the old pan-Slav dream.

Where will all this end? The French still talk of unilateral action to liberate the prisoners in the camps, and to bomb the Serbian artillery positions harassing Sarajevo. It should have been undertaken some time ago in the name of humanity, in the name of Europe, while the iron was still cold enough to grasp.

21 January, 1993

When the Victory
Parades End

It seems at first to be a question of priorities and of public relations. But behind the unpromising facade of events there lurks a much more sinister and potentially fatal reality.

The League of Nations was an organization filled to the brim with the high hopes of mankind after the nightmare of the First World War, which lasted much longer than it was supposed to and exhausted the powers of the earth. The League failed in the long run because the world recovered its breath, and after convalescence certain countries saw advantages in walking out of an organization which was not yet indispensable, but merely a court of last appeal for the wronged and the molested.

The Italy of Mussolini walked out rowdily after being condemned for its invasion of Ethiopia, lingering only long enough to jeer at the heart-rending appeal to the conscience of mankind made by the Emperor Haile Selassie.

Before an all-enveloping conflict broke out for a second time, the Germany of Hitler also noisily strutted out of the forum of the people.

Realizing the inadequacies of the League, the victors of the second cataclysmic blood-letting founded the United Nations, an organization which sought to perpetuate the high ideals of its defunct parent, while endowing it with a tougher structure.

It possesses to this day an unwieldy General Assembly of ever-growing proportions as emerging nations apply to join, and a series of Councils, the most in evidence being the Security Council. This streamlined decision-making body incorporates five permanent members, the victors of the last war, and each has an unfortunate power of veto which has had the result of immobilizing its decision-making abilities for long stretches at a time.

There were exceptions to the terrible monotony of Soviet *nyets*, but they were few and far between. When the British and French, with the collusion of Israel, had the incredibly outdated idea of invading Egypt as a punishment for its having seized the Suez Canal (a kind of mental no-fly zone of the past), the United States and the Soviet Union awkwardly found themselves as voting partners.

Before, whenever the leading powers wished to do something outside the bounds of legality, they went it alone unless, as in the case of the invasion of Egypt, they were forced back to the UN table. In the case of the US invasions of Grenada and Panama, they were over before the UN could be effectively invoked, and both the Soviet Union in its interventions in Czechoslovakia, Hungary and Afghanistan, and Israel on countless occasions, became expert at ignoring the resolutions of the UN, without ever bothering to walk out as Italy and Germany had in the past.

Today there is a great opportunity for change for the better, but as is so often the case, this opportunity is fraught with dangers. Without the Soviet hurdle, the US is now the predominant force in the Security Council, ably and consistently supported by its experienced mentors, Britain and France.

It is no doubt unfortunate, in the context of a largely developing world, that the triumvirate at the head of our planetary affairs of state represents the two most venerable and successful colonial powers, together with their brilliant pupil, who has long surpassed the ageing teachers in vigour and speed of reflex.

Up to now, the image of the UN is one inherited from the League of Nations, a somewhat amorphous place of high ideals, good intentions and benevolent feebleness.

In an emergency, it needs the borrowed strength of powerful nations to enforce its decisions. Whenever it manages to dragoon peacekeeping forces of its own, independently of the few military powers left, these are invariably elements from small nations armed symbolically with light weapons.

They are open to insult, abuse, and sometimes aggression. That is no doubt why the new secretary-general, Dr Boutros Boutros-Ghali, a man of independent mind trying earnestly to invest the UN with a positive personality it so urgently requires, finds himself booed and heckled by rabbles who have a healthy respect only for demonstrations of raw strength.

It is typical of this unfortunate state of affairs that an American congressman, on a lightning fact-finding tour of Somalia with a handful of colleagues, should state robustly that he had quickly understood what the UN had been doing there before the arrival of the US Marines. Nothing, he said. Naturally, if everything is seen in purely military terms, as is the tendency in a US intoxicated by its own efficiency, then the difficult work of UN agencies in a land dominated by the rivalry of well-armed warlords will seem relatively ineffective. But is the cure the virtual hijacking of the Security Council?

It is to the credit of Mr Bush's America that it reacted so quickly and so generously to a crying need in former Yugoslavia. But the other urgent priority selected by Mr Bush was the Gulf War, which must linger in his mind as work he was unable to finish before leaving office.

Saddam Hussein's movements of military equipment suggest a continuing unwillingness to accept defeat, and a series of sterile measures is adopted. All the old military advisers are trotted out on television, fresh as daisies, and eager to give their advice. One of them, with an answer for everything and a question for nothing, thinks that bombing will eventually compel the Iraqi people to get rid of Saddam — a theory based on the presumed reaction of an American public to a similar situation, and which has already been proved entirely misguided in a country which is not defying military might so much as flagrant humiliation.

The conflict has rapidly become one of acute embarrassment, especially when it is pointed out by a growing number of critics that 400 or so Palestinian exiles were left freezing on the rocks in no-man's land, and that the free-for-all between the participants in the Bosnian conflict goes on unabated, despite UN resolutions every bit as urgent as those applying to Somalia and Iraq.

Accusations of double standards in UN (or is it US?) priorities are fully justified. Curiously enough, Russia's voice is needed once again on the Security Council, as are those of Germany and Japan — great powers which can remind us that defeat is not the end of everything, and that victory is not always the solution. The UN must remain an arbiter, not merely a participant in initiatives not necessarily its own.

4 February, 1993

Corners to Paint Yourself Into

Many breathed a sigh of relief when Yitzhak Shamir and his party left office in Israel: they had said 'No' more often even than Gromyko and Molotov in their heyday. But now we are stuck with Yitzhak Rabin, who has donned wolf's clothing and launched one of the most ill-judged initiatives in recent history.

The arbitrary rounding-up of alleged terrorists or their sympathizers in Gaza and the West Bank, and their expulsion from Israel without ascertaining in advance whether Lebanon was willing to receive them, must be due to that usual over-confidence which is the most reliable short cut to stupidity.

It was assumed, of course, that Lebanon would give in to the slightest pressure. It invariably had in the past, from whichever direction the pressure had come. The Israeli-controlled so-called 'security zone' had been wrested from it without it being able to resist, and the Syrians were forever breathing down its neck. Lebanon was apparently a push-over which would do as it was told.

Unfortunately for Rabin, this was a golden opportunity for Lebanon to demonstrate that it was its own master, able to dictate what was permitted or forbidden on its own soil. Despite the rattling of sabres, Lebanon held firm, and the 400 or more exiles were stuck in the jagged and glacial zone between the two antagonists, deprived for a time of food, shelter and medicine.

Naturally, public opinion the world over was scandalized by Israel's callous action. It was invoked as an example of double standards on the part of the United Nations (for which read the

169

United States): so active in Iraq and so passive in this no-man's land.

The whole miserable business is symptomatic of a contemporary phenomenon. Governments with tiny majorities invariably carry out the policies of the opposition, however divergent the parties' platforms are, in order to preserve power and give policy a kind of coherence. The parties of the Left in Europe are, on the whole, only a fraction left of centre, and the inverse applies to the Right.

Unfortunately, Israel — a small country created by its pioneers and aided by the guilty conscience of the world — which started its precarious existence with the most enormous moral credit in history, has been living on its capitals instead of being content with its income. It has developed a kind of truculence which makes its friends, to say the least, uncomfortable.

Golda Meir used to believe that Arabs are just Arabs, whatever they say they are, from the Atlantic coast of Morocco to the borders of Iran, and this sort of conviction evidently fired the expulsion of the Palestinians to a neighbouring country, different only in name, which could easily absorb them.

The Gulf war, with its ruthless expulsion of Palestinians, Jordanians and Yemenis from Saudi Arabia because of differences of opinion about Iraq, is enough to show how complicated and volatile are the endlessly changing tides within the Arab world — which correspond not at all to the monolithic image that was in Mrs Meir's mind. Now sanctions are threatened against Israel by the UN Security Council. The Israeli Supreme Court responds by an offer to examine each case on its individual merits — an admission in itself that this vital prerequisite to justice had not been undertaken before.

Quite the reverse: Israel had already admitted that a handful of those suffering the privations of semi-exile had been expelled in error. Everything was now in place for one of the great botched public relations exercises in recent years.

It was bad enough as it was, but worse was yet to come. A point had been reached where the US could no longer protect Israel in the public forum, so, under pressure from its greatest benefactor, Israel came up with the daftest of compromises.

It offered to repatriate 100 of the exiles. Which of them would go home and which would stay on the bare mountain would probably have been as arbitrary a decision as everything else in this foolish affair — and this after the Israeli Supreme Court's offer to examine each case individually!

The chance of demonstrating solidarity was handed to the exiles on a plate, and they accepted the gift with good grace, declaring that either all of them went home or none at all. This news apparently came as a blow to Warren Christopher, the new US Secretary of State, who must now think quickly of another way of averting sanctions.

Eventually, of course, all the exiles will return. Israel's government just cannot afford to prevaricate much longer, and it will have to cut its losses. One trusts that Christopher will recover from his disappointment and point out to Rabin that there is no future in pretending to be Shamir — and that the peace process is far more important than a snap decision which went wrong.

But was it so very difficult to be wise before the event? Apparently. And it is that which is depressing.

Meanwhile, as accounts elsewhere in the world are being settled by gunfire, only to create vicious circles of future hatred leading to yet more tragic violence, the new Clinton administration is set to grapple with the question of — gays in the United States military.

The American political establishment features crusty elder statesmen such as Senator Thurmond, categoric to the point of total incoherence, and retired officers such as Admiral Moorer, obsessed with the alleged threat of gay bars to military morale. It is opposed to Clinton's reforming zeal on this issue, which has in effect been put on ice for a six-month period of reflection.

It is a problem which arises through the necessity for gays to admit their gaiety before induction into the armed services. This has never been required anywhere else before, which is just as well, because quite a few of the great military leaders of history would have been deprived of their victories, and their nations deprived of their services.

Can you imagine the headlines in the Ancient Greek media?

'Alexander no longer Great! Court hands down verdict! "Innocent fun" plea not accepted.'

11 February, 1993

Tender yet Steadfast

I did not know Audrey Hepburn as well as I would have wished. A long time ago, when I was a relatively young playwright, and she was an extremely young ballerina, she was brought to my attention while I was casting a small part in a play of mine which was about to go into rehearsal.

I can now no longer remember which play it was, but I do remember my reaction to meeting her. I thought she had far too much personality, which would have invested a rather reticent role with qualities it was not intended to possess. I flatter myself in retrospect that my reluctance to offer her employment at that time only accelerated her majestic progress to the top of the tree.

Much later, I was very touched to hear that she had exerted pressure on the producers of the film of *War and Peace* to allow me to play the part of Pierre. I stood no chance, despite her eloquence on my behalf, since the role had already been given to Henry Fonda, one of the finest actors in Hollywood.

But I remember her efforts with a surprise which has survived the passage of time and an affection which has inevitably grown as I was privileged to appreciate her intrinsic qualities as an ambassador for the United Nations Children's Fund.

This was a role she was not allowed to play for long, but it was one of the most remarkable of her career. I speak with feeling here, since I know how difficult it is to reconcile a reputation in the world of communciations, with all its superficial and facile aspects, with a genuine concern for the deprived and the downtrodden.

There is a rampant cynicism in that part of the world which

describes itself as developed. It would be quite prepared to understand the motives of a star willing to go to places such as Somalia in order to advertise milk powder for a fee; but it doubts the sincerity of the same star for going there without financial advantage in the service of a humanitarian impulse.

That such a state of mind exists is a reflection of the prevalent taste of our society rather than of any individual with a normal sense of responsibilities.

It goes without saying that entertaining the merest thought along such well-worn lines about Audrey Hepburn would be unjust and ugly beyond measure.

She knew better than anyone else that the recompense for such work lies in the eyes of those in need of succour. It is they who bring it home, in all its simplicity, that such work is worthwhile. Such charity acts as a little supplement to the work of those wonderful people who spend their entire time doing it. No amount of assiduous prattle in the well-fed world can ever subtract from this intimate truth.

Statistics tell us that Audrey died young. What no statistics can show is that Audrey would have died young at any age. With the perfect bone structure of her face, she seemed to possess the secret of a youth verging on the eternal, and yet the poise of maturity was already with her from a very early age.

There is no doubt that the actual contact with starving children affected her very deeply, but there was nothing overtly emotional about her ability to stoke up the embers of the public conscience. Nothing was needed other than the evidence itself and the restrained eloquence that she displayed on every occasion.

There was never anyone further away from the conventional image of showbusiness, glitz and glamour.

Nature had given her all the mystery she needed, and although her words were selected with the care of a poet, they only served to emphasize the fact that they were not merely at the service of a fine mind, but also the instruments of a tender yet steadfast heart. Audrey made a magnificent contribution to her art, and she died some way beyond the line of duty.

We sense her loss as a friend, as an acquaintance and as a personality. As an example, and therefore as a human being, she is still very much alive.

28 January, 1993

When Familiarity Breeds
Nostalgia

It is a cliché that the elderly judge contemporary life by the yardstick of a real or imagined past. Memory, they say, plays tricks, and the events of a bygone age acquire a mellow patina like antique furniture. Even the most terrible events are recollected by those who survived them with a tenderness which suggests that time itself creates reverence as it passes.

Yet it seems to me that the leaders of half a century ago were men of substance compared to the flyweights of today. Logic tells me, however, that there cannot have been as much difference as there appears, and that the way of living life itself must have changed to the detriment of those in the public eye.

Certainly the great blight of the contemporary political leader is over-exposure, which any actor knows is a misfortune almost as difficult to bear as under-exposure. Over-exposure leads to the kind of familiarity which breeds contempt for those of discernible personality and indifference to all others. Prime ministers of the past could have said more or less what they pleased in a London club, and it would probably have gone no further. Now the club itself invites the media to share their privilege and for the media, read the public.

And a remark of an indecisive and reflective nature, carefully worded to sound like a daydream rather than policy, creates tidal waves among political commentators. Is all this a little disproportionate? Yes and no.

It is normal for the onlooker to be particularly aware when watching the antics of a government which has, in soccer terms, started its match with five or six own goals. This is really a little

174

excessive to be put down entirely to bad luck.

But with the best will in the world, a suspicion of bad management and incompetence must exist, and when an idea of dole in exchange for work is put forward, it gives the impression that those in charge of our destinies are less concerned with reversing the rising tide of unemployment than with turning unemployment to their advantage.

It is a fact that the crisis in the West goes far deeper than a question of cash flow in the arteries of state, clogged by waste and made poorer by corruption and scandal. It is also, and more particularly, a crisis of self-esteem, and so of both faith and trust. Lady Thatcher never ceased to be obsessed with the idea of leadership, and Mr Bush declared frequently, on his way to defeat, that the American people were looking for leadership. Personally, I doubt if the thinking man or woman wants someone to tell them what to do when whatever it is may be contrary to individual instincts and beliefs.

If there is any novelty in the air it emanates from President Clinton's desire to be respected only as much as he himself respects the electorate. His is interesting and unusual rhetoric, and time alone will show how practical such a laudable ambition is face to face with the in-fighters of Senate and Congress.

At the moment it bears a dispiriting resemblance to the unaffected reign of Jimmy Carter, who has gained in stature since he left office. Carter's hindsight could be of use today.

With the British parliament televised regularly, there is far more exposure of the British Cabinet and the Opposition than of the American president, who is often represented by a spokesman, to save him for important occasions.

Oratory in the House of Commons rarely dignifies Shakespeare's tongue, and the puerile rancour with which past policies are attributed to political opponents today tries patience. It is without doubt the frequency with which British personalities appear on television which makes them seem even more volatile than they are.

Everything is in dire need of renewal, both in manner and matter. The French and German parliaments are both televised, the one against a background of theatrical neo-Roman pomp, the other of a no-nonsense functional decor. Neither interior lends itself to the stridency which is the hallmark of Westminster.

But one thing all places have lamentably in common is a lack of charisma among their denizens. Generosity attributes this to over-exposure, but perhaps it is as true that modern usage precludes personality in governing, and that future political life is destined to be one long yawn, with only incredible errors of judgment to awaken incredulity from time to time.

François Mitterrand is the exception which proves the rule. He governs not from the shadows but from the clouds which shroud Olympian heights. He only deigns to speak when others are silent, at times chosen by him. He says little at considerable length, and since everything he says is open to interpretation, he preserves his mystery. For better or for worse, he is the only professional politician left.

18 February, 1993

Settling Balkan Scores in a Land of Broken Promises

It is difficult to know just what is going on at the moment behind the cruel chaos in what was Yugoslavia. Yet it is not too difficult to guess — to read between the lines on the face of Mr Karadzic; to fill in the pauses in Lord Owen's guarded statements; to register his bursts of candour on a personal Richter scale; to imagine what goes on behind the mask of Cyrus Vance's insistent cordiality to all and sundry.

There seems to be some urgency for general acceptance of an extremely complicated scheme for dividing Bosnia up into regions, depending on where its inhabitants wandered at the time that they were all getting on well, or, at least, had better things to think about than murder, rape, and other contemporary means of self-expression.

But will this plan, produced under pressure, be better than that of other peacemakers at the end of the First World War — those who created Yugoslavia, adding recycled debris salvaged from the Austro-Hungarian empire to Serbia and Montenegro? It looks, in retrospect, as though the wise men of long ago lumped these disparate elements together on ethnic and geographical grounds in the belief that because they were all Slavs a degree of harmony was guaranteed.

Religious wars were things of the past in 1918. In a continent supposedly purged of its foolishness by four and a half years of the most terrible warfare ever, it was not thought that it made much difference that a new kingdom contained Catholics, Muslims and Orthodox Serbs. The gamble looked as though it had worked, despite an undertone of conspiracy which never quite left the Balkan scene.

Only the multiple convulsions of the Second World War brought into the open all that had been hidden. This suited the Nazis, who, on finding it impossible to pacify or even fully occupy Yugoslavia, resorted to the old and useful theory of dividing in order to rule.

They created a puppet state in Croatia, which helped them police the territories which they managed to hold. The Croatian Ustashi maltreated Serbs with a brutality which shocked even the Nazi SS, and horrified Italian priests who returned to Rome with accounts of hair-raising excesses by the Catholic Croats against the Orthodox Serbs.

At the end of the war, the communist virus spread rapidly through eastern Europe. Tito emerged as a great leader from the high mountains, from which Yugoslav partisans had created nightmares for the invaders. His reputation was ready-made by events, and his charisma and ferocious taste for independence ensured that Yugoslavia was not sucked into the Soviet economic system.

Tito's relative isolation between the capitalist West and the communist East gave his nation an importance out of all proportion to its military and economic strength, and pressure from outside assured its integrity. After Tito's death the country held together from force of habit. It needed an external event to imperil the nation.

The event was the explosion of the Soviet empire, with fallout far beyond its borders. Suddenly there was nothing to protect oneself against, and time to remember that there were old scores to settle. Scores against the Croats for ancient cruelties; the Muslims for 400 years of Turkish occupation; the Albanians for having spilled out into the cradle of Serbian civilization, the region of Kosovo. Everyone in the region found they had long memories, and there was suddenly no lack of pretexts for spilling blood.

So in what way can the peace plan put forward by Lord Owen and Cyrus Vance improve on the post-1918 territorial realignment?

The Croats accept it as it is, for the time being. The Serbs, who feel wronged by western attitudes to them, accept, with many vague and inconstant conditions. These resemble a conditional refusal as much as a conditional acceptance — and if that seems incoherent, it has to be, as it reflects as faithfully as possible the various Serbian positions. The Bosnians reject the plan out of hand, since they are the great losers in it, and claim that it does nothing to punish the perpetrators of ethnic cleansing.

The Americans seem to be backing the scheme, after a delay marked by evidence of Lord Owen's impatience, for which he was rebuked by the *New York Times*. The fact is that he is now entrusted with most of our hopes as well as all our fears.

The US believes the plan might have to be altered to make it acceptable to all sides, and it does not rule out the military option. The Russians do rule out the military option, and think the scheme is fine. Europe looks from one to the other in undignified perplexity, while its lightly-armed troops are exposed to arbitrary dangers in a landscape full of ugly surprises and broken promises.

Whatever the merits or failings of the Vance-Owen peace plan, it will certainly not be binding in the long run. Settling these accounts has no finality, and sooner or later they will be opened again for re-settling. In such a context, signatures mean nothing. In this knowledge the Serbs and Croats may well be tempted to sign.

The Bosnians, however, fear that whatever it says on the document, it may well be their death warrant, condoned by our paralysis.

25 February, 1993

Even Corruption isn't What it Was

Only a person with a stony heart could avoid having a soft spot in it for Italy. It always riled Mussolini, a man with a very Italian gift for self-delusion, that his country produced waiters and maître d's in such profusion and of such universally accepted excellence.

Somehow it suggested to his mind that brilliance in a profession entailing culinary organization reflected on the country's image as a military power. As so often among dictators, he confused service with servility. They are not at all the same thing. In fact, being a private soldier in an army fifty years ago came far closer to servility than does the average waiter, who takes pride and pleasure in his work.

If the Italian has a fault it is the evident desire to give pleasure — and his intention to share in that pleasure. There is no doubt that the classic British butler, carefully enunciating the words 'Dinner is served, my Lord', takes equal pleasure in his prescribed task, which entails successfully disguising whatever satisfaction or uplift he may derive from it.

Different peoples have different ways of taking pleasure in their own way of doing things. Today these various ways of reacting to events are all under pressure as rarely before in history. The Renaissance followed the Dark Ages simply because there was no other way for civilization to survive. Today we are faced with a situation quite as dramatic, and where the discovery of a new direction for the human race is as urgent as ever it has been.

There is even an unusual cordiality between politicians of various nations, driven into warm relations by their shared unpopularity. It has been a period of indifference towards candidates by voters. A weariness at the same old faces relying on the same catchphrases and a rise in inspired puppetry on television — the only form in which many people can still swallow their daily dose of politics. As if these infallible gauges of public apathy were insufficient there is the rash of major financial scandals involving banks and brokerage firms which have spread like a contagion throughout the developed world.

Italy, for instance, is engaged at the moment in the most thorough spring cleaning ever indulged in by a coherent nation on its own body politic. Every day brings with it several resignations from high office and at least as many arrests.

Several months ago the then Italian president, Francesco Cossiga, resigned for reasons which seemed obscure. With the passage of time the reasons are becoming crystal clear, implying that he was the only one to see the oncoming tempest with a clear appreciation of its destructive force.

The fact with which the nation is now faced is that the whole structure of society is permeated with corruption, as a noble building may be pervaded by dry rot. It is evidently difficult to imagine a total absence of corruption in a land in which the Mafia has long been a model of organized efficiency, especially when compared to ministries and other public offices shackled by red tape. Now it is a matter of honour for the police to show themselves to be the equal of the Mafia in steadfastness and imagination. They seem to be succeeding at last now that the Mafia has sickened public opinion by its indiscriminate murders.

At this point, it is interesting to try to define corruption. I suppose that tipping a head waiter before a meal is corrupt since the diner expects special treatment in return for his investment, whereas the same sum slipped into the head waiter's discreetly cupped hand after a meal is merely gratitude, for services rendered and therefore not corrupt. A fine enough point probably to start an argument in court.

Suffice to say that when I produced a film in Italy in the late 1940s I needed certain permits. A meeting with the minister himself was arranged. An Italian contact told me that the gift of a Parker 51 would be much appreciated. I was appalled. 'I can't go in there and give a minister a fountain pen!' I remonstrated. My contact's eyes became steely, his words clipped. 'He is expecting it,' he said. Shyly, I gave the minister the pen before a word was exchanged, thus making sure that it would be recognized as corruption in the time-honoured tradition.

The minister was beside himself with pleasure, and I got my permits. It was quick, efficient and painless. But what has happened to corruption since, not only in Italy but in the world? It has become swollen-headed and megalomaniac, and suffers from incurable inflation. It no longer gives pleasure to all concerned, as in Italy in 1948.

Today it gives momentary intoxication, headaches, and, with luck, long prison terms to reflect on what went wrong.

4 March, 1993

One Step On, but How Many Back?

The European desire for aggrandizement has burst its banks and spread over the face of the globe under a variety of hypocritical pretexts, such as that of carrying truth to people who have found peace and harmony without it. But it is salutary to remember, from time to time, that it was not ever thus.

Meek tribes are waking up to the fact that their colonizers not only robbed their ancestors of their birthright, but forced on them disease and alcohol in exchange for literacy in languages not their own.

Now, at least, slavery is a thing of the past. But there are still restless movements of peoples across borders — borders which bigots describe as sacred — imposed by the development of nationhood.

Peoples in search of food, work and safety are as disrespectful of frontiers as animals — and rightly so. Just as the present is under continual bombardment from history, which resents change and progress, so history itself is under continual pressure from pre-history, which is oblivious to the planting of flags and other symptoms of greed and possessiveness.

There are reminders of the endless growing pains of this planet everywhere you look. America was colonized by various pioneers, none of whom seemed to know what they were doing. All they knew was why they were doing it.

After landing in *terra incognita*, some of them thought they were in Japan. When the English, over-cautious and late as usual, heard of the success of Christopher Columbus, they decided to acquire an Italian navigator of their own. The secret weapons of the time seem to have been Italian navigators.

The settlers from Europe were stronger in the reading of Holy Writ than in the reading of compasses. John Cabot landed in Canada some years after Columbus's success, sure that his discovery lay south of Columbus's landing place. King Henry VII was delighted with the new acquisition, wherever it lay geographically. It turned out to be Newfoundland and the grateful monarch pressed all of £10 into Cabot's hand as a reward.

African slaves were brought to America, the Caribbean and Brazil for menial work in the plantations. These days, human conscience has overcome the weight of ignorant prejudice. The chief of police in television series is inevitably black nowadays and the Chief of the American Combined Staffs is also black. Evolution is indeed taking place — at least on one level.

The painful and moving transition from the degradation of apartheid is another instance of man's courage in influencing his own destiny.

And then there are the sudden landslides in parts of the land-scape thought of as solid granite. The collapse of Yugoslavia, previously considered an evolved society of mixed, if comple-mentary, cultures, has now plunged the region into a dark age more primitive than we dare admit. Our horror at the events can only match our disappointment that such a reversion is possible. Sooner or later the warring parties must realize what a nightmare they have allowed themselves to slip into and how hopelessly out of step they are with the laws governing human behaviour.

Unfortunately it takes a great calamity to stoke a twinge of conscience into action, and we have to live through apocalyptic events in order to conjure up sufficient stamina to rectify them. Human impulse is immediate; human redemption as slow as a prison sentence. When a life is lost we also lose a sensibility, an intelligence, a unique viewpoint. Life has never been dear enough. There are still hundreds waiting on Death Row, the penalty of lazy societies on those who have strayed outside its rules. Death is the final out-tray of all our bureaucracies, what Hitler would have called with his characteristic inaccuracy 'the final solution'.

The city of Florence, where I find myself, is a microcosm of all humanity. This majestic place, so redolent of humanistic and artistic glories of the Renaissance, is still today an accurate mirror of all human tendencies. Mass migration takes place as much today as it did before. The extent of Chinese infiltration can be judged from the growth of Chinese restaurants in the city.

In the main square a marble plaque commemorates Savonarola, the macabre monk whose right-minded sermons offended highly-placed men. He was burned at the stake nearly 400 years ago together with two followers who volunteered to share his fate.

Man, slow as ever to see things in proportion, has at last reacted with contrition to this excessive act by the Borgia Pope. And so it goes on slowly, gradually, one step forward but how many steps back?

11 March, 1993

Liberty can be a Dangerous Drug

Oh liberty, liberty, how many crimes have been committed in your name? The last time this great phrase was uttered was by the French Marshal de Lattre de Tassigny at the end of the Second World War. The priceless vineyards of Burgundy had just been liberated and the Allies were pressing on into Germany. Elements of de Lattre's advance guard found to their joy that most of the great vintages at one of the most renowned vineyards had survived the war.

De Lattre decided to hold a dinner in honour of the Allies' liberation of France. When the sacred wine was served, an American general explained to the gathered throng of top brass: 'Unfortunately, there was insufficient wine for everyone to drink a toast — so our resourceful support staff have made it go further, with medicinal alcohol.'

It was while lifting this polluted beverage to his lips that the horrified Marshal de Lattre de Tassigny muttered the famous phrase. Since those heroic days liberty has been subjected to as many abuses as ever — even more by those who profit from it than by those who would put an end to it. Liberty is not only something to yearn for when you haven't got it; it is also too easy to take for granted when it is a normal condition of life.

Take America, the Land of the Free: a land of high ideals and brilliant achievements, but also one where the unrestrained exploitation of freedom, as though it were mineral wealth struck in a backyard, erodes men's sense of proportion. To the point where some, with a literal interpretation of the Bible, hear a voice on the crossed line from heaven instructing them to slaughter innocents. With the kind of arrogance encouraged by the concept of the sky being the limit, casual, even multiple, murders are committed. Liberty is seen as licence.

Yet the crazed behaviour of individuals is nowhere near as significant as the subtle exploitation of liberty by those in important positions. In Italy we can see what happens when corruption becomes so much a way of life that it is almost indistinguishable from normality. One reason for heightened sensitivity to scandals involving dishonesty on a high social level is the worldwide recession. In times of affluence and exorbitant spending corruption is often hardly noticed — indeed, it can seem an essential grace note in the hymn to plenty. When the tide suddenly turns, however, we inevitably become conscious of a dangerous imbalance in society.

There are bankruptcies, fraud and scandals; a spate of golden handshakes. Most of us are less immediately affected by these abuses of liberty in high places than by the shocking plague of individual failures and unemployment among our own circle. There is nothing more calculated to awaken the anger of normally good-natured people than to be suddenly plunged into penury while still surrounded by the apparent wealth of others.

All these anomalies and risks are inherent, like microbes in the lifeblood of liberty. Is liberty, then, a bad thing, to be avoided? Of course not. Liberty is the essential ingredient in the life of a balanced community — but with the luxury of liberty, human responsibility increases immeasurably. It is a form of adulthood: a normal development from the servility of the classrooms of doctrinaire regimes.

At this moment Italy is a perfect example of an adult assessment of the ravages of the cancer diagnosed in its entrails. The man in the street is rightly outraged by the abuses which have impoverished the taxpayer and benefited the privileged, but his attitude is generally rational and constructive, with a balanced instinct for the possibilities for both good and evil in mankind.

In much of eastern Europe, problems are now down to the most basic level: survival. This does nothing to improve the frame of mind of those eager for the kind of reforms which will ease the burden of life, not aggravate it. How long can people live on promises as a substitute for daily bread? Is it any wonder that there is, in the minds of the sceptical, a desire to whitewash past communist regimes; to think of them as something that half worked, and therefore preferable to what doesn't seem to work at all?

Already Lithuania has voted communists back into power. They have never entirely left Bulgaria, Romania, Slovakia or, indeed, Yugoslavia. Elsewhere they wait in the wings. These peoples have already learned in a hard school a sense of responsibility towards the community. Let us hope that when liberty comes at last, as it is bound to, they will not lose that sense. Liberty without responsibility is the most dangerous of drugs.

18 March, 1993

In Retreat From Reality

When presented with a weekly column to fill in a respected newspaper, the temptation is to deal in a personal manner with the latest insult to reason that has been served up piping hot in the world's headlines.

If the present trend continues, one can imagine the sorry figures of UN peacekeepers, miserable infantrymen from Madagascar or Laos, watching helplessly from their white battle-wagons as French farmers in Boulogne spread mashed potatoes over highways, or rabid fishermen from Grimsby douse thousands of fish with petrol. The image is too awful to contemplate, especially with the spectre of famine forever gnawing at some outskirt of human life.

With gunfire prevalent from every point of the compass, be it the streets of Bombay, the landscapes of Texas, the foliage of Angola or the snows of Bosnia, one has the impression that the only people expressly forbidden to shoot are the apostles of non-violence, the UN peace-keeping forces. They might almost better be described, owing to their impossible mandate, as war-watchers.

How this folly will end is anyone's guess. Therefore, forgive me dear reader, if I turn to tiny observations on the grind of existence as a momentary change of pace.

Together with some colleagues, I have been engaged in a six-hour television series on the history of the Vatican, a fascinating subject which is far away from the ugly realities of contemporary life, and yet, by virtue of its juxtaposition of men and organizations, full of historical parallels.

189

The quest started in Rome and has since taken us all over the north of Italy, and will now move on to France, Germany, and Turkey. To be plunged into medieval Italy is certainly a sabbatical from contemporary turmoil, although, surprisingly, it lays one open to the same irritations which must have plagued those who lived long ago.

For instance, Sunday is reserved as a day of rest in the Christian calendar. But try to sleep late after a taxing week in Assisi. Those confounded birds which so eagerly engaged St Francis in theological banter are hard at it. At 4.30 in the morning they begin, a celestial chorus so deafening that it is a miracle that St Francis was able to get a word in edgeways.

At the very moment that the birds stop, the bells begin; from little carillons from wayside chapels, sounding like duchesses ringing impatiently for the next course, to great sonorous peals which set up throbbing reactions in the ear.

On Monday the restaurants are open again, and one of the leading ones, bearing a tribute to St Francis in its name, has canaries in cages shouting their little heads off all evening. No doubt it is the drift of civilization which has consigned them to cages, a sad commentary on the saint's colloquy with liberated nature.

There is a tendency in Europe for ancient cloisters, castles and even prisons to be converted into hotels by imaginative entrepreneurs. There is no shortage of raw material of this sort in Italy. One can even foresee an age-old reformatory becoming a luxury hotel of the future, proudly bearing a plaque announcing that the entire Italian Cabinet once slept here. Such places usually vary between those of modern luxury lurking among the antiques, and those which try to give you an authentic taste of medieval discomfort.

We stayed in one of the latter category. A magnificent door in my room, with opaque stained glass and a key worthy of a chastity belt, opened on to the wall, its function being purely decorative. The same could not be said of the shower fixture, which came out of its socket in its entirety, falling on my head while my eyes were full of shampoo. It must have looked like Laocoon fighting the sea serpents as I struggled to capture the showerhead. It snaked away from my soapy hands as streams of scalding water went everywhere but on to my hair. The bed was vast, but had deep trenches in it which awakened a suspicion that quite a few cardinals had died there and even lain in state.

One curious fact emerges as the tale of the Vatican unfolds. The *cognoscenti* deem Toulouse-Lautrec and Bonnard to be the first great painters to grace commercial art with their genius. But we can see that they had precursors in the field of propaganda — not for a commercial product, but an entire religion. Michelangelo, Raphael and Leonardo da Vinci all worked on a commission basis, turning out Madonnas and Child. Crucifixions, Resurrections and Annunciations.

O.K FELLERS. HERE COMES ST. FRANCIS... ON THE DOWNBEAT, I WANT UNRELIEVED BIRDSONG TILL THE BELLS START

To be honest, after surveying cathedrals and churches full of these, the pagan sophistication of the Birth of Venus comes as a breath of rejuvenating air.

Now we are in Avignon. The murals are mostly workaday by Italian standards, but the superb small hotel, La Mirande, is a return to discreet comfort, and miraculous gastronomy. Television is back after our Italian abstinence. All the modern icons are here too, from Cyrus Vance to Slobodan Milosevic.

What has happened during our retreat? Frankly not much. Perhaps the Italians have a point after all.

25 March, 1993

Of Faith, Fear and Forecasts

There are, of course, exceptions. There always are. But on the whole, religion is essentially a matter influenced by climate and geography. It is as difficult to visualize a great Catholic procession with its extrovert symbols of faith — papier-mâché effigies, hooded penitents and golden crosses — north of the Arctic Circle as it is to imagine a Protestant sermon — casual and confidential — delivered amid seas of flickering candles and soaring baroque angels in a Mediterranean land.

Every religion is very much a reflection of a culture and a way of life. In some instances, as in the case of the fundamentalists, it purports to be an entire way of life, but in more sober societies it is content to be a condiment which gives its particular flavour to existence. To travel, as I have done, from Rome, through variations of dissent at Avignon and Wittenberg (where I find myself at this moment), is to feel these sea changes acutely.

Rome, like so many human manifestations which appear monolithic is, in fact, a glorious city with a more than chequered history: it has known defeat, occupation, humiliation and desecration as well as triumph. Enough, at least, to earn it the description of Eternal.

It is still there, long after the last Barbarian has gone: a maze of pagan ruins and Christian shrines, having been an amalgam, sometimes difficult, of temporal and spiritual power from long before the birth of Christ. Just as the year knows its seasons, it has known decadence. There have been midsummers of rampant vice and cupidity, followed by deep hibernations of the spirit.

At times, it seemed as though most goblets had a few drops of

poison in them. Never mind. Above and beyond the embarrassment of the Borgias (with their shameless appointment of boy
cardinals and other absurd abuses of power, and the burning at
the stake of Giordano Bruno and Savonarola for reasons which
today seem specious, to say the least) there was always a con-
stancy, a continuity, about the Church which is impressive — a
determination to survive.

Emperors and kings, both Holy Roman and French, often lost
patience with the Church's pretensions to be a spiritual guide
without the means to enforce its guidance militarily. Philippe Le
Bel, King of France, even went so far as to kidnap the Pope in
order to teach him a lesson. As the Pope was old, he died as a
consequence: that was the lesson he learned. The general consensus was that the king had gone too far, but the result of this
action was the setting-up of an independent papacy at Avignon,
which lasted more than three-quarters of a century.

All the Avignon Popes but one were Provençal, men from the
immediate region of Avignon, and they lived in considerable
style in their new palace. They made the city a bustling nouveau-
riche centre of commerce during the period of the ersatz papacy.

St Catherine of Siena, a woman of inflexible force, who rein-
forced vision with visions, was instrumental in luring another
aged Pope back to Rome, and for a time there were two Popes
— until Avignon was forced to give up under the moral weight
of its venerable rival. The Papal Palace of Avignon looks bare and
forbidding today, and no wonder. For many years it was used as
a barracks.

Napoleon continued the tradition of secular insolence by having himself crowned Emperor by the Pope, seizing the crown
impatiently from the Pontiff's hand and placing it on his own
head. Many liberal spirits with high hopes in Napoleon, the
First Consul, were bitterly disappointed by this surrender to
vainglory. Among them was Beethoven, who tore up the dedication of the Eroica Symphony, supplanting it with the cryptic
phrase: 'In memory of a Great Man' — a sombre epitaph to
the immediate past of one still living. Simon Bolivar, who was
present at the coronation, ostentatiously turned his back on the
procession.

But these were mere ripples on the surface. A far greater threat
to Rome's pretensions to universality occurred at the very beginning of the 16th century, when Martin Luther unwittingly set

CONFOUND IT. I'VE JUST THOUGHT
OF A 96TH THESIS

the Reformation in motion by the paradoxical means of accusing the Pope of being an imperfect Catholic. It follows that, had the Pope been a perfect Catholic in Luther's eyes, there would have been no Reformation — at least, not at his hands.

An outstanding target for Luther's misgivings was the then prevalent habit of selling indulgences, or pardons, which meant that the richer sinners could reserve numbered seats in heaven on condition that they paid the Church in advance. This practice seemed to Luther's Catholic eye a denial of Christian ethics, which he saw in the final analysis as a matter between God and the individual exclusively. He pinned his famous Ninety-Five Theses to the door of the church, inviting discussion and correspondence. They are splendidly objective, and as truculent as was his character.

Number twenty reads: 'Christians should be taught the Pope's pardons are useful as far as one does not put confidence in them; but, on the contrary, most dangerous if through them one loses the fear of God.' The desire not to be outrageous is evident. Whether it is successful or not depends on one's point of view.

Wittenberg, a small town southwest of Berlin, was a famous seat of learning of huge dimensions for the time. Its university, founded in 1502, was still very young during Luther's heyday. He occupied the chair of moral philosphy.

The place is mentioned in *Hamlet*, and was the scene of Dr Faustus's legendary pact with the Devil. Lucas Cranach, the painter who did Luther's portrait, was known as the richest artist of his time, by virtue of being by far the fastest. He was also Bürgermeister of Wittenberg.

After Luther's time the town declined, eventually passing from Saxony to Prussia, which finally put a lid on its dreams. The famous university was shut, sharing the fate of the Papal Palace at Avignon by being turned into a barracks. In 1935 it flickered momentarily into the public eye when a large factory making explosives blew up, earning the voluble commiseration of Hitler. Then, after the war, it vanished into the grey bosom of East Germany.

Today it stands a little like a seabird shaking the effects of a brush with an oil spill out of its feathers. There are still vague traces of soot in the air — that odour that used to plague us all and still pervades parts of eastern Europe. And yet, in the very short time since the collapse of the German Democratic Republic there are already palpable changes, and they are considerable. Food is plentiful and the culinary arts are practised skilfully. Despite depressingly high unemployment, everyone appears to be quietly busy. Old buildings are refurbished, new ones built.

But is it in any way a counterweight to Rome? By contrast, yes. It is not a place of majesty; a showplace of devotional achievement — but that was never its mission. Did not Luther object to the cost of St Peter's basilica in Rome, paid for in part by those notorious indulgences? Wittenberg is a place of thrift, of fiscal accountancy, of moral accountability.

It is cosy in Luther's chambers at the Augustinian monastery: a panelled room dominated by a square table. Here he sat with his wife, a renegade nun, and his wedding guests, most of whom, like himself, were under sentence of death. They were far enough from Rome not to be burned at the stake, yet close enough to be remarkable for their courage. Today the ancient quarrels are wreathed in smiles, in Rome and Wittenberg, at least. They share goodwill and an upward gaze. The rest is history.

1 April, 1993

Wild Swings of the Compass

And so the French voted massively for the Right. It looks like a tremendous change, but will it be? Was the outgoing French government, in fact, one of the Left? Is the Spanish government, which has lost popularity since coming into power — as all governments whatever their tendency invariably do — a government bearing all the characteristics of socialism? Is Her Majesty's opposition in Britain as far to the Left as its Conservative detractors claim? What is Yeltsin's true position in a country in which the conservatives are the communists and the believers in freedom for the individual are the equivalent of the radical Left?

The questions are endless. One of the few clear facts emerging from a world too well-informed for its own good or at least for its own peace of mind, is that the public are unwilling to believe, after decades of catastrophe, that most politicians are even half-way competent.

The result, which politicians regard with the same anxiety as rock stars scrutinizing the hit parade, is a dangerous drop in the number of those casting their votes.

Some nations, like Belgium and Australia, seeking to suppress this possibility by frankly undemocratic means, compel their citizens to vote. With all due respect to these countries, in many ways exemplary in their tolerance and pursuit of liberty, this is neither constructive nor fair as a solution to the problem of rising public apathy.

Not to vote is not necessarily a sign of laziness or lack of civic sense. It may be an expression of opinion. And as such, it deserves the respect accorded a vote for a candidate.

What is it then, about the present state of affairs which has tempted the public to be so reticent? It may well be the enormous amount of television air time devoted to political debate, programmes in which politicians confront each other, or else are asked searching questions by journalists or selected members of the public, and during which various well-oiled techniques for avoiding direct answers, or making counter-accusations, are boringly evident. But possibly the underlying and cardinal reason is that the lines of policy between existing parties are now blurred beyond recognition. This is due to the diminished range of possibilities in a future dominated by the necessity for economic survival and co-existence on a planet so shrunk that every nation is the virtual neighbour of all the others.

Doubtless the reason for the temporary eclipse of what is broadly known as socialism is the fact that idealism has become a word associated with financial mismanagement and hopeless centralization. In truth, financial chaos is quite possible without the burden of idealism. Privatization has not in every case been the answer to the constrictions of nationalized industry. Bureaucracy is neither created by governments, nor destroyed by privatization. It is set in motion by size, and size alone, existing everywhere where administration is uncommonly large and lacking the possibility of a human dimension. Size encourages somnolence and indifference, whether in empires as gigantic as the ex-Soviet Union or in vast corporations like General Motors.

It is curious, nevertheless, that communism, which once seemed so modern and Utopian, aged so rapidly. Admittedly, when it was an established force, and in direct competition with the industrialized West on the most sinister level, that of nuclear arms, or in the far reaches of space, it managed to keep abreast for a while. But on the much more important level of everyday life, it fell far behind, not only in its achievements but even in its dreams.

Albania, twenty years ago the most communist of all lands, quarrelling with the Russians over questions of orthodoxy, and eventually with the Chinese for the same reasons, was left alone in its own miserable immobility, unable to envisage anything beyond the range of its own postage stamps, which displayed a steam engine pulling its carriages through a nebulous landscape under a canopy of smoke; a steamer belching clouds of pollution into the air as it confronts the open sea; and a worker waving from the seat of an antediluvian tractor with its starting handle very much in evidence.

Communism was defeated by progress — not merely technical progress, but social progress as well: the developing intelligence and self-respect of the common man and woman despite all the influences and bluster they are subjected to, whatever regime they live under.

Today, the conventional compass points of Left and Right have largely lost their significance. There are fewer and fewer of the landed gentry and colossal inherited fortunes left, while a generous glut of crooks and chisellers have taken their place. The most glamorous cars are no longer driven by dukes or chauffeurs, but by men so unused to wealth that it must be visible. As for the working class, it is only a reality in the oratory of old-time socialist leaders with memories too long for their own good. The working class has been replaced by the unemployed, and they are, for the time being, classless.

The situation which confronts us is no better and no worse than what went before, it is merely different. Because it is different, it cannot be judged by the standards of the past.

The French think they have voted massively for the Right, or against the Left. And yet, at the solemn yet cordial takeover handshake between the outgoing prime minister, M Bérégovoy and the incoming prime minister, M Balladur, it was M Bérégovoy who was smiling broadly and M Balladur whose smile was small and pinched.

They are both experienced enough to know that from a moment of victory there is only one way to go, however gradually, and that is down, as the public tires of the same old faces and the same old phrases.

As for the opposition, free from the irksome business of governing, they are able to entertain ideals once again on the long, slow ascent to power, so tempting a mirage, so grim a reality.

8 April, 1993

Singular Help for Plural Suffering

This is a report from the ante-chamber. The ghastly conflict in Bosnia, so tragic and so absurd at the same time, goes on without so much as a flicker of humanity. High technology demonstrates its capabilities in the skies round the clock, while officers from another age travel to and fro between the places where they give orders to rape and shell. They sit around conference tables where they discuss ceasefires they have no intention of keeping.

Everyone seems to agree that the complicated plan hatched by Lord Owen and Cyrus Vance is far from perfect, but they add that it is better than nothing. Is it?

If it is no improvement on the solution of 1918, then it will not be a permanent settlement of an old issue, but rather a signal for the resumption of barbarities once the peacekeepers have left.

Until then there can be few destinies more frustrating than that of a member of the peacekeeping force. Their gallantry and courage are put to the rudest test by their enforced reticence under the most irritating provocations.

I said that this is a report from the ante-chamber. Conductor Georg Solti and the Slovene mezzo-soprano Marjana Lipovsek organized an Easter Sunday benefit concert for Bosnia as part of the Salzburg Festival. They asked me to moderate the concert, whatever that means, and I was honoured to accept.

I drove towards Salzburg from Munich during the Easter exodus. In the traffic there was one terrifying vehicle, a coach once white but now pitted and covered with rust and mud. The wheels shook precariously as they revolved around hubs which had long metal rods protruding from them, Boadicea-style.

Barely visible on its side was writing in the ultra-modern style of the 1930s, spelling out the words Srebrenica Ekspres. Empty, it was probably going back for more refugees. It made me realize that Austria is the ante-chamber on the edge of the outrages, and a haven of civilized values, such as its deep concern for its former province.

In those days there was a catalyst, Archduke Franz Ferdinand, whose assassination in 1914 in Sarajevo set off the First World War. This time the preference is for artillery aimed not at the scion of a royal house but at people in general.

And the great powers, with the First World War still in mind, are wary of involvement in a difference of Balkan opinions. Instead they demonstrate their technological superiority in the belief that such supersonic arabesques in the sky will impress those who know that none of these implied threats will ever be carried out — unless there is a faux pas on such a scale that it makes a punitive move inevitable.

A remarkable woman in Austria, Karolin Wendt, a psychotherapist, decided to take matters into her own hands. She carried relief work into Bosnia itself. Warned by the Austrian Foreign Office not to drive to the war zone, she did just that. Today she has settled in Zenica, a Bosnian town with a normal population of 85,000, swollen to more than 200,000 by refugees.

She attempts to repair the psychological damage to those subjected to physical damage such as amputation. She has a clinic devoted to children rendered dumb by trauma, such as being forced to watch their mothers raped. Her initiative is called 'Help and Joy'. And there are others, such as 'Neighbours in Need', to say nothing of 'Trade for Aid', the idea of a young Swede I found standing by his white six-wheeled truck, purchased from the Austrian army, and preparing to drive back into the war zone carrying supplies and ingenious ways of keeping minds busy and constructive. His assets are a bank overdraft and boundless optimism. It is wonderful that such people exist at a time when more and more is expected from individuals and less and less from organizations. An exception to this rule is the superb Berlin Philharmonic Orchestra, who not only played without remuneration for this best of causes, but donated their considerable fee from a 17-nation Eurovision hook-up as well.

Naturally the soloists and the conductors Solti and Claudio

Abbado did likewise. But cannot even more be done?

Whatever it was should have been done long ago. It is curious to remember that in more blood-thirsty times half-a-century ago, the staple question to alleged pacifists at the conscientious objectors tribunals was: 'How would you react if you saw your sister being raped by the enemy?' It was assumed in those gallant days that the enemy had better taste than to rape your mother. What would the answer be today?

Perhaps this: Register your complaint with the nearest UN post and, while awaiting instructions, convince your sister to take courage from the daily fly-past.

22 April, 1993

Moments When it Pays
to be Blind

A lover of sport will instantly recognize the importance of initiative. Any match of any sport is a struggle for the high ground, the imaginary-geographical feature which causes one competitor or one team to dominate, and the other to submit, or at least merely to react.

To complicate this truth further is the factor of stamina, the fact that it is a physical impossibility to take the initiative for longer than physical or moral conditions dictate, which means that once the opposition is worthy, the competitor with the momentary initiative must continually worry whether this has not been taken too soon to earn a victory.

In the murky pages of human conflict, there are many examples of those who recognized that initiative was a vital ingredient in success. Nelson knew exactly the moment when the initiative had to be seized, even by methods not exactly orthodox, to free himself from the dead hand of those who submit to orders from above or to *force majeure*.

Admiral Hyde Parker, who did not give his name to the recreational zone any more than he gave his name to anything at all, but who happened to be Nelson's immediate superior, signalled by means of flags at the masthead that he wished the fleet to withdraw from the waters before Copenhagen. When this order was brought to Nelson's attention, he is reputed to have raised his telescope to his blind eye, saying: 'I see no signal,' and proceeded to win the Battle of Copenhagen. Of course, had he lost the battle, it would certainly have led to a court martial, but as it was, the Admiralty was willing to overlook such disobedience.

It must be added that Nelson has two advantages over other mavericks. The first is that he made it a habit to win victories, and the second is that not everyone has only one eye.

Now comes the case of General Morillon, the French commander of the UN peacekeeping force in Bosnia-Herzegovina. Here is an officer faced with a task twice as difficult as those confronting Nelson. After all, he only had to win, or, at worst, not lose. General Morillon's mandate is to do neither, but merely to be there as commander of a symbolic force, which must somehow preserve its morale under the double onslaught of an enforced impotence and being the observer of terrible abuses.

He looks liked a grounded Commander Cousteau, and it is easy to read on his lined face the depth of his concern. He belongs to the race of those who take initiative as opposed to the dull majority content to react to events imposed upon them. He detached himself from his command and vanished for a while alone into the battered town of Srebrenica, thereby retaking the initiative from the Bosnian Serbs, who up to then had enjoyed an easy monopoly of it. He was armed only with his moral authority, and his witness was the world. For a while it seemed as though the trigger-happy and those without conscience had found more than their match in this solitary, soft-spoken figure. It was too good to last.

Rumours began to fly, and to be contradicted when it was seen that certain facts would be unpopular. It was said that he would soon be replaced. The UN added that such a change was a purely French matter. The French talked of routine changes. M Leotard, the new French Minister of Defence, visited Bosnia dressed in khaki fatigues. Whatever the outcome, the Western allies have successfully neutralized a welcome breakthrough into another dimension of debate, and consigned the concerned onlooker to the same ongoing nightmare as before.

Meanwhile ex-President Bush is received rapturously in Kuwait, which is as it should be. Whether that war was just, or indeed justified, is still an open question in many minds, so skilfully was the handling of the press, and so bland the employment of the Security Council in the pursuit of unanimity.

In those days they taught us to be blood-thirsty by demonstrations of sheer efficiency at work, bridges being bombed, breathless pilots reporting modestly, even charmingly, on their direct hits. The errors only came to light later. In Bosnia it is all

THE MILITARY OPTION, THEN AND NOW

FIRE!

TAKE COVER...

error. Gone is the silly ecstasy of battle. There is no affectionate American general to take us step by step through the campaign. There is, in fact, no campaign. Just chaos, punctuated by perplexed UN soldiers taking cover from stray bullets and going where they are allowed to go.

And all those who were so keen to show the flag, or at least the cheque book before, are now full of pious appeasement. When Lady Thatcher raises her voice again in the House of Lords, expressing thoughts which can only be embarrassing to Europeans with an interest in the future of the continent, she is inelegantly set upon by Mr Malcolm Rifkind with his air of an outraged hen.

Morillon and Thatcher are both people who, rightly or wrongly, think for themselves. In other words, they are of those who know initiative when they see it, and are not lacking in the courage to be different if public opinion is adrift and prey to dangerous currents. They have nothing to learn from the Rifkinds and the Leotards of this world, who for the time being have merely attained greyness in their quest for eminence.

Despite difficult times, Europe should have taken an initiative in ex-Yugoslavia a long time ago. Now, it is both far too late, and extremely urgent. Many tears have flowed. It will not end without more tears, many of them. They will be due not to our foolhardiness, but to our timidity.

29 April, 1993

Fit For an Apparatchick

Chemnitz is hardly a name to conjure with outside Germany. During the existence of the German Democratic Republic it was called Karl-Marx-Stadt. One of the first acts of reunification was to restore the original name to this centre of textile and other industries, which was savaged by air raids during the war, like Dresden, some 80 km away.

In Chemnitz, after the fall of the Berlin Wall, Marx's statue was not toppled from its plinth to join Stalin, Lenin and other socialist-realist worthies on the refuse dump. This was because his bearded cheeks and leonine mane already reposed on the sidewalk: a blackened angel with the prescience to have fallen to our level before the troubles. I have never lingered long enough to discover whether the huge effigy is of bronze or granite. All I know is that to reach my hotel I have to turn left just after it.

But what am I doing in Chemnitz in the first place? Well, Dresden, a city in full reconstruction after the atrocious wartime destruction, is understandably eager to put itself back on the map as a great cultural centre. For its first festival after its rebirth, it sought local partners to help spread the cost. Chemnitz, a community without great international pretensions, was the logical choice, as nearby Leipzig was too much of a rival.

On the face of it, Chemnitz had few assests. Unemployment and the lack of capital were neither better nor worse than elsewhere. What does exist is a high regard for cultural values. The outer shell of the old opera house survived the raids, but inside everything is new. The orchestra, called the Robert Schumann Philharmonic, which performs in a lovely new concert hall, doubles up as the opera orchestra and is of superb quality.

So much is written in the western press about the uniform and unredeemable miseries of the East that it is easy to believe every allegation, and I must say I arrived well indoctrinated by what I had read. Until, that is, I saw a spanking new yellow Ferrari parked outside the hotel. It had Chemnitz number plates. I asked a local: who could afford such a vehicle in streets still full of malodorous two-stroke Trabis? 'Oh,' came the answer, 'it must be one of our new rich.'

The town is recuperating almost visibly, but old habits die hard. Many of the young to middle-aged speak Russian, since it was the second language taught in their schooldays. And the operas I am preparing for the Dresden Festival are both Russian, sung largely by singers from the Bolshoi and other Russian opera houses. Some of the singers still live in Russia; others have found havens as far afield as Massachusetts.

Working with these artists is as rewarding as it is amusing. It is usually necessary to curb their verve rather than to inspire it, but they are all avid for fresh experiences and gifted with tremendous technique.

In this connection I recollect a meeting with an elderly east German couple in Salzburg, for the first time outside their native land, by coach tour. They marvelled at the opulence of the Austrian shops, the cleanliness of the streets, the sheer efficiency. All they missed was what they referred to as a certain human warmth. It is undeniable that in parts of the world where life has been hard, there is necessarily another dimension to friendship.

The 'human warmth' was a compensation for a host of disadvantages and even follies. The hotel I mention is perhaps a symbol of what went before. A massive pile designed in 1930 by the famous Dessau Bauhaus, the launch pad for so many celebrated architects, it was a model of functional beauty half a century ago. It is still an extremely pleasant building, but often compromised by the extraordinary concepts of luxury which must have tickled the fancies of apparatchiks. On every guest's pillow is a message from the new owner, Herr Gönnewig, apologizing for the fact that he is still awaiting permission to bring the building up to date, and requesting the client's indulgence.

This Herr Gönnewig is an engaging character. Owner of some twenty-two hotels and restaurants, mainly along the Rhine, he purchased this architectural landmark only to find himself prevented from carrying out any renovations. Doggedly, he has decided to stay in Chemnitz until the situation is clarified in the courts. If his lawsuit fails, this excellent hotel risks becoming a historic monument of a different sort.

My bed is made of massively solid oak, with sections of glass let into the bedhead. The bedside table and the footboard are decorated with blue bubbles and fractured bits of blue glass imitating rock crystal. The lighting is indirect and dim, from flickering strips either very close to the ceiling or very close to the carpet. The motif of bubbles and rock crystal is carried into the bathroom, but presumably because of the proximity of water, the baleful light struggles out of portholes. It is extremely difficult to shave successfully under these conditions.

The sitting room has a sofa which is set around three sides of a vast table, and is massive enough to have found its inspiration from the thrones of maharajas lodged on the backs of elephants during a durbar. This sofa would have needed several elephants to move it, with room for eight cronies of Herr Honecker, each seat separated from the others by tubular armrests as hard as bags full of bricks.

Here, I feel, as I sit alone of an evening watching television, is where senior comrades closed their eyes in rapture behind protective hedges of carbonated water and tallboys of boiled sweets, knowing that to be here at all they had *arrived*.

I wish Herr Gunnewig good luck with his lawsuit, but if he wins I shall miss the marvellous absurdity of the room I occupy. He deserves the last word: 'If these people accept the novelties we bring them without losing what they have already, they will unfailingly reach the heights.'

6 May, 1993

Old Men, Young Spirits

The news has been awful this week. The bleak events in Bosnia have dominated, while here in Germany a strike began, in search of goals which seem an echo of solutions long abandoned elsewhere. How did this bastion of stability ever bring itself to take the huge step backwards into the tetchy realm of industrial disputes?

It is on this generally depressing note that I decided, for once, to ignore the tendencies of the day and to write an optimistic piece about the curious process of growing old.

On the face of it, this subject seems to have as little to recommend it as an analysis of the present recession, but there are redeeming features. In fact, it would be unfair if ageing were seen entirely as a decline of the faculties, culminating in the permanent immobility which the experience of our ancestors has led us to expect.

One reward which was unexpected in all this is the gradual realization that the human soul may well be immortal, even as the human body begins to submit to its evident mortality. It needs no great religious awakening to come to such a pleasant conclusion, merely a realization that this body we are stuck with, and which was not of our choosing in the first place, began life as a *fait accompli.*

Gradually, however, it begins to acquire the characteristics of a rental car, something at our disposal which is subject to the passing of the years like everything else, and therefore of slowly decreasing efficiency. It has to be driven more and more carefully.

And the human soul in all this? Ah, it is the part of us which never ages, which retains the spirit of the heyday even if its orders go unheeded. For instance, tennis used to be one of the joys of my existence. Today I can no longer trust my legs to carry me rapidly in the direction of the ball, but this in no way impairs my mental appreciation of what is going on as I watch others play.

On the contrary, my theoretical grasp is much more thorough than it used to be, so that I can anticipate when certain shots spell disaster, and applaud all the more fervently if a stroke of genius turns defeat into unexpected success. In other words I am of an age to be an expert, one of the battalion of boring fogies who dominate sport by their frequently erroneous decisions.

Some time ago it was suggested that I might like to be a linesman at Wimbledon. 'We need someone of your enthusiasm,' I was told. I excused myself by expressing myself flattered by the offer, but begged them to renew it when my eyesight had deteriorated sufficiently for me to be able to make wrong decisions with absolute conviction. In case this column is read by those who issued this invitation, I hereby inform them that the time is now ripe.

After all, with service speeds in excess of 200 km per hour, I might as well join those fine ladies and gentlemen who struggle to their feet, scurry across the court and point imperiously to a trace left by some other ball in a previous rally. To add to the confusion the umpire then descends to examine yet another trace born in his imagination only to decide the point must be played again, to the fury of the player who made the winning shot and the silent satisfaction of its exonerated victim.

Eventually, linesmen, faced by the extraordinary speed of the modern game, will be eliminated altogether and replaced by computers, which have the virtue of being capable of errors far grosser than human ones, but which are not open to appeal. Public hoots and whistles are lost on them. There is not much time left before the twilight. I am not foolish enough to identify myself with whatever the underdog of the day might be, but I am fully qualified to be a fallible, somnolent and obdurate linesman.

There are dangers of another kind attached to the eternal youth of the soul. Every time I invite one of my daughters to dinner and we enter a crowded restaurant, I am conscious of the stares of other diners. Occasionally I catch an eye during the journey to the table.

Expressions vary from the acidulated, suggesting amazement that the old fellow is still at it, to undisguised hostility, proclaiming either a deep-felt disgust at such a mismatch, or even, perhaps, a burning jealousy. All this is of course vaguely flattering and I often find a smile of grim satisfaction on my lips which seeks to confirm the worst fears of others.

This is merely a case of innocent mischief, but whenever old men behave badly, it is invariably their youthful souls which fail to realize, either mistakenly or deliberately, the extent of their physical decrepitude.

It is this depressing fact which creates so called 'dirty old men' whose watering pupils dilate with every passing cleavage or quivering buttock. Dirty young men are encouraged, even solicited, in public, where they are described with some relief as normal. Dirty young souls inhabiting ancient carcasses are quite a different matter. They are bad taste, deserving of compassion in generous natures, but then the onlooker rarely sees further than the visible facts and merely registers revulsion. The gradual decay of the inhabited body hardly exercises the mind in the normal course of events.

But certain catch phrases begin to make surprising sense: 'unsteady on the pins' and 'long in the tooth' both refer to facts which are abstract in the youthful, but which become real with the passage of time. Also the skin above the eyes begins to sag like heavy drapes.

But none of this — the throat resembling a loosely strung guitar, the unexplained twinges and quirks in the joints, the lack of breath on stairs — are considerations of more than momentary importance. The soul, the lessee of this impermanent residence, is as young as ever it was and will be.

20 May, 1993

Frailty Paraded in Public

What is confidential? What is secret? What is open to investigation? What is taboo? In the old days, the highly-placed used to be able to get away with murder, or so it was imagined by those bereft of influence by birth.

Certainly, the number of scandals avoided by the quick-thinking of those on the spot is most impressive by the standards of today. A French president, Félix Faure, who is still revered today, died while making love to a lady in his office. Being a truthful man, he had told his wife that he would be working late. Death struck at a moment of rare ecstasy, with the result that *rigor mortis* set in almost immediately. His fist clenched a mass of the lady's auburn hair, and no amount of tugging and cajoling would persuade it to let go.

In those days, security held no sinister connotations as it does today, and the only man on the spot to hear her screams was a doorman on night duty, who, with brilliant foresight, fetched not a policeman, but a priest.

The priest turned out to be a broad-minded fellow, who helped the doorman release the by-now hysterical lady from her amorous vice, and even painstakingly removed the tell-tale hairs from between the suppliant fingers of the corpse. Then he muttered the words of Extreme unction before doing his bit in restoring a presentable appearance to the distinguished casualty. Only when a fountain pen had been forced between the petrified thumb and forefinger of the right hand, and the head carefully lowered on to the blotting paper, was the widow informed that her husband had passed away while his hands were actively engaged in steering the ship of state.

Those were the days. This is one type of event capable of evoking what the French call a *raison d'état*: in other words, something so intrinsically damaging to the state that an unexplained silence is fully justified.

There are countless other examples of this. In America, Warren Gamaliel Harding was no great shakes as a president, but was still able to maintain a mistress within the White House — one of the few successful initiatives of his incumbency — while J. Edgar Hoover, the founder of the FBI, and an unscrupulous terror to the open-minded, was recently alleged to have been a notorious transvestite. He was able, it is said, to appear at reunions of kindred spirits dressed as a nimble dowager. The fear he inspired in others was apparently able to ensure the total discretion of those able to penetrate the disguise.

In England, Prime Minister William Gladstone's predilection for attempting to lead ladies of the night into the path of righteousness was known but suppressed. His motives were never questioned, even if some detectives responsible for his safety may have had their doubts.

At an earlier date, the Borgias in Italy were able to behave in a way deemed outrageous today without even the tiresome need for secrecy, simply because they were in a position to do so. The heritage continues to this day, as Italy's drastic measures against corruption testify. Only the other day, the mysterious death of a leading French politician's son-in-law was announced as a dramatic news item, but remained wrapped in complete silence subsequently. No reason was given. There was not even an element of mystery. So hermetic was the discretion that the public recognized the shadow of the *raison d'état*, and understood that it was of benefit to nobody and of disproportionate pain to those involved for the facts to be dragged into the open. This event has now receded into oblivion.

By and large, however, things have changed fundamentally, not always for the better. America is inevitably the style-leader in the quest for openness, and all others have obeyed the call with varying degrees of success. There have been resignations from public life for many reasons, nearly all of which would have been accounted insignificant a century ago.

In America, where the tendency is to subject potential holders of high office to a minute and often preposterously finicky public cross-examination, purporting to assess the fitness of the candidate for the job, the test is invariably one which merely judges his or her ability to box clever.

Recently, the dogged refusal of a potential Supreme Court judge to crumble under the pressure of evidence of sexual harassment volunteered by a former employee was a rare example of determination rewarded. No amount of tasteless questions from senators could dent the applicant's serenity, and he passed the test with his reputation as intact as possible under the rules of these procedures. He has been a model of discretion ever since.

Quite a few distinguished senators have come under merciless scrutiny from their fellows, and have ended the worse for wear, while the procession of ladies hoping to occupy the highest legal post in the land was remarkable by virtue of their admission, one after the other, of having been guilty of minor improprieties many years ago. Did they think they could bluff their way through this inquisition? If not, why did they apply for the job at all? Suffice to say that the lady who eventually occupied the coveted office was proved to be without blemish, but it was she who made the decision to storm the stronghold of the religious fanatics in Waco, resulting in lamentable loss of life. In line with the contemporary fashion for moral masochism, she took personal blame for the catastrophe, thereby disarming any possible criticism. Justice today is as air-conditioned as is the atmosphere, and about as healthy. Everything is a matter of consensus, and experts abound to give their advice.

She did not make the controversial decision to storm the stronghold alone. She consulted a psychiatrist and a social psychologist as well as the police and the military. And out of all this extended palaver came a singular failure, which brings us automatically to another aspect of the *raison d'état*.

America is a large country, in which even the smallest problems tend to grow in size. The events in Waco immediately captured the public imagination, and forces were mobilized which satisfied expectations — tanks, bulldozers and the rest.

Then it lasted too long. The forces of order were the first to become edgy. The self-styled prophet, David Koresh, kept the initiative by changing his mind endlessly. God's messages to him were indistinct, and the huge posse camping on the windswept plain became the victim of this crossed line to Heaven. Tempers began to run short. The delay was as embarrassing as the fact that

216

the size of the rescue operation carried no weight with the beleaguered fanatic.

No one knows the advice of the psychiatrist. It is well to remember that Radovan Karadzic, soft-spoken leader of the Bosnian Serbs, is also a psychiatrist, and one can imagine what his advice would have been. Whatever the advice of abstract experts, the truth is that every step was televised. Every punch was telegraphed in order to fuel public interest. If the beleaguered garrison had television, they could follow every move of the opposition, and the preparation of every surprise. We know the result.

MR. KARADZIC ASKING
US TO BELIEVE WHAT HE WOULD
HAVE SAID HAD HE BEEN ABLE TO
AND WHILE WE'RE ABOUT IT, ARE
THERE ANY FURTHER QUESTIONS FOR
ME TO DENY ?

More recently, in Paris, a similar drama took place. After a few days of silence, during which every demand of the kidnapper seemed to be fulfilled, a spare commando of a handful of men moved silently in and killed the guilty party, frightening the children, but in the best of causes. There were American complaints at the time of a lack of information. In an age in which justice is commensurate with entertainment, there is a good case to be made for the *raison d'état.*

The Americans invented the phrase that nothing succeeds like success. Nothing fails like failure either.

27 May, 1993